The Poor Man's Impenetrable PC Fortress

By Thomas "Einstein"

2nd Edition

I0475910

Table of Contents

Other Resources:
- School Issued *Microsoft Press* Certificational books.
- Any of the *Using Microsoft Windows* books
- *Stanford University - Secure Computing: Best Practices for Windows XP* (was actually removed some years ago!)
- *MS Windows Command Ref.-* WndCmdRef.chm - 1,877,623bytes
- *Ten Windows Services, You Don't Need.* March 17, 2008
- …Finally, *Computer Security Guide For Paranoids* By Paladin Press has to be a good read just because they published it.

Chapter 1 - Preface

Around the late 90's, a antitrust lawsuit against Microsoft was being dragged on and who ever watched the movie *antitrust* around that same time? It was loosely based on Microsoft's "scandal" and how they use and abuse genius employees. Toward the end, its revealed the fictional *Janus* operating system had an ulterior purpose and the fictional company's founder, was a nerdy part time hacker who would order hits on ex-employees who got too close to the truth... And In real life, i dont know what's true and how much movie dramatics actually happened but the backdoors in operating system software, whether legitimate or not, are really there. Now with smartphones, tablets, and those other platforms like Apple, Chrome, etc, there are probably several different Januses out there. No, Microsoft isn't the only big name anymore but with its software development going back decades, isn't going away nor should it.

This book is intended to guide you how to setup and manage Windows in a cost effective manner... and be free and secure like a personal computer should be. The first step is to freshly install Windows on your PC. Next, all the needed adjustments to Windows are covered. Software top picks are described in one chapter (and maybe even included). There is also chapters on windows management and network settings, and further on an important section giving tips on not falling prey to honeypots, bait 'n switch or misleading websites, hacker tricks, and how to remain less obvious while web surfing. lastly, throw away those free trials of big name anti-virus/firewall products, I'll show you how to firewall Windows using NT's built-in tool of the trade.

The appendix section, among other things, contains many useful MS commands and shortcut keys that any true PC power user should already know.

Much of the problem is because there is so much confusion and red tape around Windows. I will try to explain. For decades now, Manufacturers and MS had a deal worked out. The *OEM act* allows them to mass distribute Windows with their brand of machines. Your software license is paid for when you buy a new computer. The Certificate Of Authenticity (COA) tag is a holographic sticker tag on the back or bottom of the computer. That tells the product key and what Windows edition its licensed for. Think of this as 1 Windows license.

Then **Fair Use** says you're allowed to use your computing device any way you see fit as long as you're doing nothing wrong or unlawful like distributing ripped movies to the world before they hit the theater. The computer and all its memory and storage contents are yours.

Almost every retail computer for the past 2 decades comes with MS's software license - the COA tag. Dumps are chock full of e Waste items like broken computers and all these have tags. So, If you have lots of junker computers laying around, you probably already have lots of software licenses for various editions of Windows 98/2000/Me,XP,Vista,7, and so on. And if one of your broken computers in the junk pile just happens to be the exact same brand and model # they can't say diddly crap. Suppose you had

Windows Vista or Windows 8 and wanted to downgrade to XP or change from Vista to 7 or from Windows 8 To 7, and already have the license's product key and a friends Windows 7 disk, no problem. The point is that if you can go dumpster diving for software licenses then you win the argument.

Chapter 2 – Backup and Reinstall Windows

Stay away from that generally accepted myth that more updates and antivirus software will fix your computer. The solution and second step to eradicating all viruses/malware/rootkits or any other thing compromising your computer's HDD is to clean install the operating system. If you have any important data, **do a backup first**! i'm betting that you can manage the backing up files yourself **without any special software.** Drag & drop valuable files in no time to a USBv2 or v3 drive. **Further on in chapter 4**, i have helpful tips on doing a organized and complete manual backup.

My advice about re-installing with Vista/7/8/9/10 - The first Windows upgrading frenzy happened in 1995, or about 20 years ago when users were going from Windows 3.1 to Windows 95. With some exceptions (no pun), everyone found their computer just ran too slow afterwards, and then it gets worse. A screwed up Windows 95, was not uncommon. Everyone had to spend lots of money for computer service and upgrades or just plain buy a new computer. This cycle of *upgrade hell* has repeated ever since. Today we hear nightmare stories of forced upgrades to the latest Windows. Windows 7 users are not immune and its in jeopordy to getting messed up for unknown reasons. It has 3 times as many background tasks, runs way slower, and is very inflexible. You might say, "but i have to use software where the minimal requirements is Windows 7..." fine, you won't get the full benefit of the poor man's approach but still might be better than what you had.

The steps in this guide were tried and tested on XP but many of the settings are still doable in any Windows editions. I won't be covering anything about forced UAC, run as Admin, Network diagnostics wizard, Aero View, or any of the snazzier GUI stuff, or even newer policy options, and so on.

Re-installing with NT / 2000 / XP - The steps below are almost exclusively for 32-bit XP. Unless you have something better... Windows XP runs with as little as 133MHz, 128MB RAM, 5GB HDD. This version of Windows worked so well in fact that they never matched its performance since. Windows 7, dubbed the better Vista, is the best of the worst, and still is horrible. The thing takes forever to startup, to sleep and a quick hibernate is not even a option. They been forcing upgrades on users while putting high security on activation of the supposedly inferior XP, and don't get me started on that. Your validated, so what's wrong? Here is steps to enjoy a more stable Windows experience while getting around those barriers.

You first need the following:

- PC computer, with no operating system, and the minimum requirements for Windows.
- Drivers for this computer (if no recovery discs)
- 2nd working computer to download stuff with.
- Windows installation disc (we'll go over this later on)

You might also need:
- File-sharing software.
- The manufacturers recovery discs that came with your computer when you bought it.
- Generic Windows installation disc
- A internal/external writable CD drive + blank discs.
- A decent flash drive. 2GBytes is minimal size nowadays.

Backup Important Files
Before you go any further, you need to decide where to save those important files. Depending on your circumstance, your files need to be copied from and then probably to a final destination into a offline archive – that means another hard disk, burning optical discs CD/DVD/BluRAY, tape backup, NAS,or even just a large capacity thumb drive for temp storage.

You may already be thinking complicated backup utilities, something about a rule of thumb, save everything you possibly can, make several incremental/differential backups every so often, etc. In reality, backup utilities are not required. You just need to organize your files; just like a file cabinet full of papers. Prioritize – which items are most important and where do they go? Chapter 4 will help you and will explain *installers* and why you can't just backup already installed software. Backups can be as simple as booting your old computer and copying a few important files to a USB drive. In extreme cases, your computer of interest may be inoperable because of software problems. In which case you just remove the tainted(but working) hard drive, hook it to a working computer as a secondary(slave) drive, and copy the important files off of it. How you hook that drive up depends. Desktop hard disks are IDE if older, or *Serial ATA,* and hopefully yours allows at least 2 drives hooked up. Unless its SATA, there's no compatibility between older laptop and desktop hard disks unless you got a special adapter. With backups to USB, time is an important consideration. How good is the bus speed? Does it even have *USBv2*? **More in chapter 4 on doing backing up.**

Install & Activate Windows...

- **Generic Windows XP Pro/Home disc** - The standard Windows disc, whether its *Retail, OEM, Acedemic, or Volume License Edition* comes with one major caveat, getting activation. You only get 30 days to use it. Now they sell new Windows XP discs published under another big company name, not MS. So, it's version might be re-designed a bit.

- **Manufacturer's recovery disc(s)** - The software that came with your computer is a sure thing. This could be as one or more discs. The first(or only one) will have Windows itself. Others contain drivers and additional software. Some computers might only have a onboard recovery partition. It might have options for burning recovery disc or booting at startup by pushing a special button. Recovery discs come loaded with extra software you may not want. After booting and installing these discs you first should uninstall/remove the trial versions of anti-virus (like Norton, AVG, McAffee, whatever) and then any other software that doesn't look native to windows and automatically resides running after startup. Additionally, go to Start menu > Run... type msconfig.exe<return> and remove all startup programs and maybe even services that had anything to do with the software you just uninstalled. It might be a lot of extra effort but at least get the anti-virus stuff out of the picture first or you could have problems making settings as administrator further on. Reboot and now you should be all set.

- **A Windows Distribution** – besides credible computer techs making their own installation discs for clients, these have been floating around in the file sharing/torrents scene. I think *Windows Black Edition 2014***(687,590,869 bytes)** is the best yet. Comes as a disk image that can be burned to bootable CD. All it is, is a stripped down 32-bit XP Professional w/SP3. Includes extra drivers, SATA compatible, NET updates, software like Firefox browser, performance tweaks, and the crack wont fail after a time either like the older black editions... there you go.

- **Building Your Own Windows Installation Disk** – Microsoft has always secretly published instructions on deploying unattended installations for corporate licensees. Imagine being able to create your own Windows Installer... Total files cannot exceed 700MB. You also need .ISO software for burning your own boot disc. One good and well-designed software product is *MagicISO*. other FREEer alternatives are *nLite* and ISOrecorder.

- **Windows 2000?** - Besides being phased out, its almost as good as windows can be, right? Has all the essential features of a NT operating system.

- **Windows Vista/7/8/10** – Most people only do a upgrade for the same reason they get antivirus software - after their computer's software has been screwed up beyond belief. Updates, virus fixers and the rest of the quick fixes, are only temporary solutions to the underling problem of poor computer management. But if you do really want the latest, don't piss around with the expensive (one time?) *upgrade* deals! If you really want to clean the slate, do it right and get the whole Windows installer disc. You have rights to this! Do a full backup and clean install then learn some safer computer habits next time.

Obtaining drivers - You will need drivers unless your using the recovery disk that came with it or the computer is REALLY old. signs of lacking of a video driver is screen redraws are much slower, less resolution modes available only. And a missing audio driver, you get no sound at all. Computer mfrs. may have a support section on their company website that lets you get specs., manuals, and most of all the drivers for any specific computer based on the model #. Use the exact name, model #, or even service tag of your machine. (for 32-bit Windows XP or not) - Download just the drivers. any utility software is usually unneeded. You should at least have drivers for most of these:

- Chipset
- Audio hardware, stereo speakers(sometimes including microphones and line in, certain modems).
- Video Hardware
- Ethernet network device (NIC)
- Wireless/WLAN (w/bluetooth) network device
- Internal modem

Optional downloads:
- Touchpad or mouse
- Firmware updates
- Utilities, applications, and add-on tools.
- Bluetooth utilities and drivers
- Micro/SD Card readers
- Web camera

Download each that best matches your exact computer and d/l all if there is more than one driver for any particular device (like video, audio, network, etc) and you just don't know what it is. By the way if your computer is for vista or windows 7 & up, and you can't find those XP versions of drivers, then you might still luck out. Do some cleaver searching online and see if someone else has already done the downgrade or some smart individual reworked the .inf files to be compatible with xp. Look into *driverpacks.*- **Keep a backup of drivers should the manufacturer decide to drop support for your old PC.**

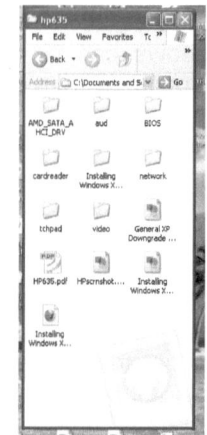

Put drivers, manuals, and screen shots neatly away in a folder, then on a thumbdrive for using after installation.

Installing - Hook up to your computer - only the essentials (power, keyboard, monitor, mouse). DO NOT plug in any Internet at this point. Turn on computer. Make adjustments in the BIOS if needed. Go into BIOS by typing the special key, like F2 or something in POST mode.(when you first start machine). Ensure the boot order allows you to boot from CD. Put windows disc in CD drive and boot computer and type a key when it asks to boot from CD. Wait 5 min. and just follow the instructions. Delete all partitions in most cases, create a new partition and even a extra partition if you like. format it NTFS or NTFS(quick). wait more and if this is just a generic windows CD you are using then windows installment wizard is going to ask you more things along the way. This is called 'babysitting'.

Problems that could occur are as follows:

- **Conflicts with recovery partitions** - Windows system should always be on c drive. Some newer machines come preinstalled with a special partition and you might need to wipe this recovery partition to install XP correctly because of drive letter conflicts. Make sure your ass is covered here and save these recovery files if possible. If you have a extra hard drive then just simply swap hard drives.
- **Computer doesn't recognize CD boot drive** - The boot priorities/order needs to be adjusted in BIOS.
- **Windows doesn't recognize hard disk** – This is likely to happen when downgrading a computer because plain old Windows XP doesn't recognize laptop SATA drives by default. You need to go into BIOS and change a setting called something like ACHI or legacy hard drive compatibility mode. If BIOS doesn't have this HDD

compatibility setting, you'll have to slipstream in the proper SATA driver by creating a new installation disk with nLite(see above).

- **Some other malfunction** - Something here might need fixing or wires checked, etc.

Windows installation walk-through:
Note: Some or most of the steps below may not be present if you're using a manufacturer's recovery disc.

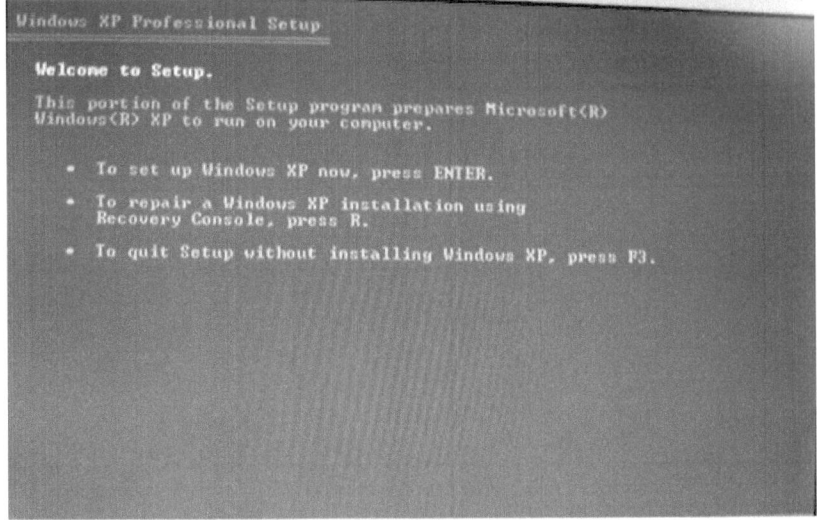

The first menu you should see after inspecting system.

Next thing is after this is the EULA. Hit F8 to continue and then go on to delete and create partitions. The computer then formats and proceeds installing windows to the hard drive. In another 10 or so minutes, the computer reboots and continues loading in windows. You should be able to use the mouse at this time. Soon it asks you to confirm locale, time/date, and time zone. click next when done and it will ask you for a product key. Enter this and click Next...

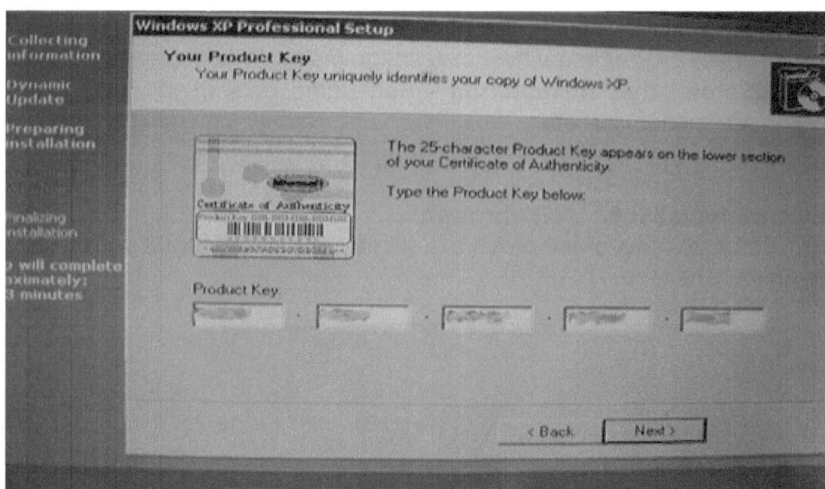

Enter a working product key here to continue.

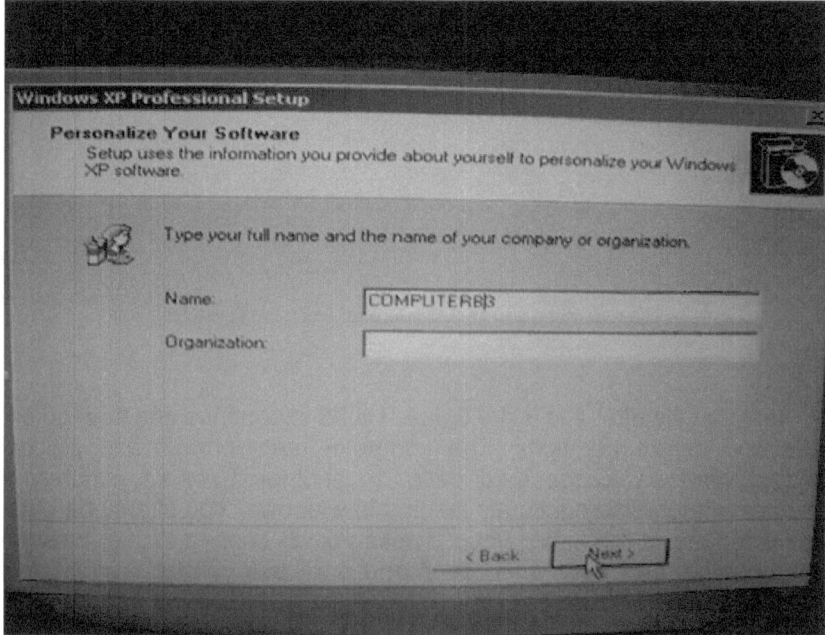

Put in a name here.

12

Windows XP Professional Setup

Computer Name and Administrator Password
You must provide a name and an Administrator password for your computer.

Setup has suggested a name for your computer. If your computer is on a network, your network administrator can tell you what name to use.

Computer name: `COMP1234`

Setup creates a user account called Administrator. You use this account when you need full access to your computer.

Type an Administrator password.

Administrator password: `••••`

Confirm password: `••••`

< Back   Next >

The Computer name is the name that identifies you in a TCP/IP and NetBIOS network. You must also give your admin account a password to continue.

...After installing windows, you should be left off in your user account...

Account User's desktop

13

At this point you can see if windows is already activated or not.
- Go into Start menu > All Programs > Accessories to see if 'Activate Windows' is there or else wait 10 minutes and see if a little key symbol pops up in the notification area (lower-right corner).

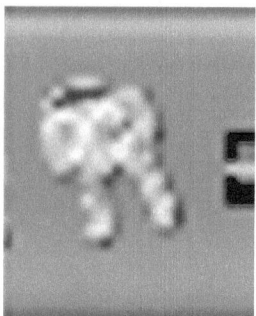

If you see this, windows is not activated and you should take care of that ASAP.

Optional - Copy D:\I386 and D:\support directories from cd drive IF YOU CAN - before removing installation disc, copy these folders to C: drive This will save you the step of having to insert the windows disc to install additional windows components if that's ever a problem. Whenever it asks for it, change d: drive to c: and your done.

Your Administrator account - In addition to your user account, You need a administrator account. Windows provides a built in administrator account called 'Administrator'(home edition has one but its only reachable in 'safe mode'). You can create your own admin account if necessary. This is where you work offline, install carefully chosen software, make changes to windows setting, check logs, set the time, or set the privileges of the other user(s), allow or not allow access to directories or files by other users, or do any other management to your system. The administrator account should be treated with care, no double-clicking executable files or scripts, avoid going online, avoid using web browser online. Your admin account should see hidden files, system files, and file extensions.

Your User account - Think of this user account as your general use, rough and dirty, abuse it as you see fit account. Websurf those funky online places to your hearts content. Its hard to get trojan horsed when as a User or Guest. You cant even access critical files or make system-wide changes. And when a general user account does get infected, just delete it and start a new one. You get to have as many user accounts as you like - each with their own private file space. For this chapter, your User account should be promoted to admin temporarily. This is needed to perform a few settings. Finally, you lower its privileges so you don't compromise your whole machine using it.

14

Initial steps

- Go to User Accounts. Click Start menu and then click Control Panel. Double-click 'User Accounts' (this is also called 'nusrmgr.cpl'). Click *change the way users log on or off* and deselect welcome screen and fast user switching gets greyed automatically. Ok out close out of this when done.

- Verify that you now have both a User account and Admin account - names are arbitrary and you can call these anything you like. The Admin account should have a password.

- In standard XP pro, log out of your User account then log into Administrator. In Home edition you'll have to create your own admin acct. first.

classic logon window lets you go into the administrator account.

Changing the looks and the Folder Options settings - First, do this to whatever account is to be the administrator. Open any windows explorer(go to start>my computer>c: for example) then adjust the look of this to whatever you like by going to menu item 'view' and selecting between thumbnail, tiles, icons, details, etc., resize the window till its the way you want then go to tools>'folder options...' and on the view tab click 'apply to all folders'. There! Now every explorer window will at least have smaller icons(The default is big icons) Next, go back to tools>'folder options...' and the view tab and uncheck 'use simple file sharing' then check 'show hidden files and folders' and uncheck 'hide extensions of known file types' and 'hide protected OS files(Recommended)', agree to the resulting popups, and click apply or ok. Now you will see filenames + extensions (everything after the last period) so someone who knows better can see what file association will

15

be invoked if a icon were double-clicked(opened). You'll also see transparent looking file icons, like *thumbs.db* sometimes when navigating through folders. Those are your system files or hidden files.

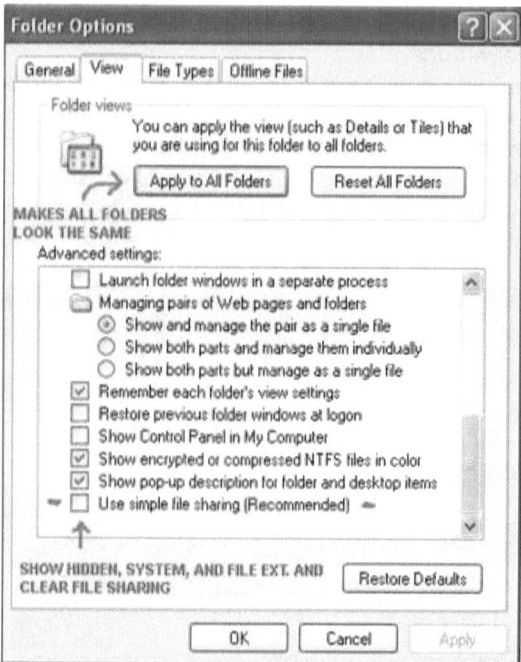

Show extensions, hidden and system files, turn off file sharing, and apply views to all folders.

Your admin account is for serious business. Change the desktop background. Go to display properties and on the desktop tab set the wallpaper to none and choose a real boring single color for the background. For any web browser, turn off any and all plug-ins, add-ons, javascript, java, flash, and anything like that – **Admin's web browser should never go online.**

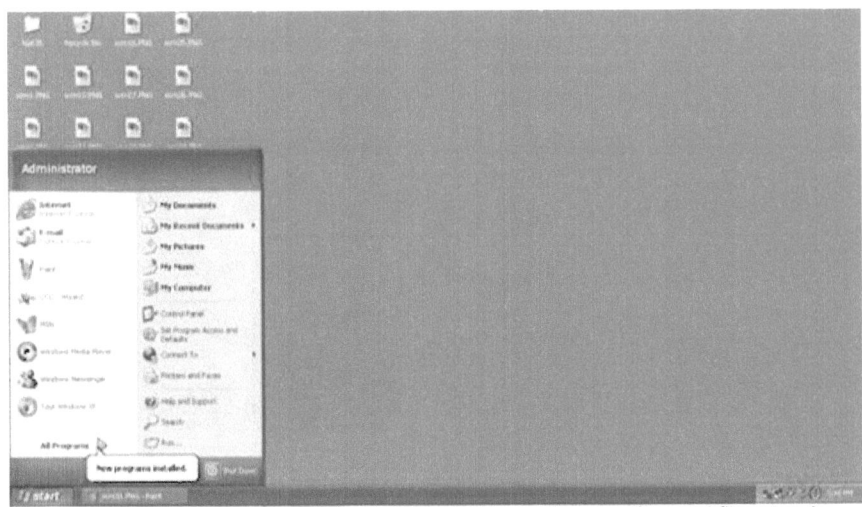

Your admin account should now be able to see hidden and system files and file extensions.

Installing Drivers

Now that windows is activated and ready to go, Using your flash drive, copy and install all the drivers that you downloaded online (or otherwise acquired) earlier. They say you should install the chipset driver first. Once all drivers are installed, check for sound, make sure video is improved or any screen resolution improvements, and look for evidence of NIC and WLAN adapters. You might have to lastly reboot. Touchpad mouse support, if installed shows up as a notification area icon.

Tip: Some older computer drivers(before 2005) including IBM computers might also need to be executed after the installer runs(since you're not using the automated recovery cd). look up the folders the files were installed to, find a setup.exe or msi file and double click that(run it).

Sometime drivers fail to install properly, then you have to install the .inf file manually in the New Hardware wizard. Whenever you have a driver problem like this, open up Device Manager, or run 'devmgmt.msc'. Find the uninstalled device, right click it, and choose 'Update driver'. You then get the New Hardware wizard. Opt out of automatically search for driver and then choose advanced or to go look for driver yourself. Finally you should see a 'Have disk' button and that opens up a browse file to supply the needed driver .inf file. Refresh device manager and scan for changes to see if the driver has taken.

Disable tapping on a touchpad mouse(optional) - First of all, tapping is a annoying feature that causes you to click things you don't mean to. The whole reason for needing the touchpad driver in the first place is just to disable this unneeded novelty. Navigate to the tapping setting and uncheck it in most cases.

17

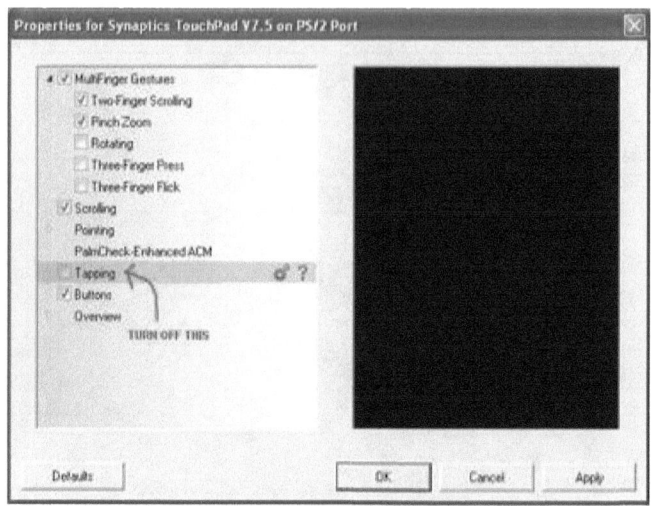
Synaptics and alps software is needed just to disable tapping

Installing Service Packs/Updates - If you don't have Service Pack 3 already, Its called WindowsXP-KB936929-SP3-x86-ENU.exe. its size is 331,805,736. Run this as admin, wait 30 min., and you're done. Other than SP2 and SP3, i'm not a believer in automatic updates. Even if its stressed about by so called experts to install all the 100's of hotfixes. The exploitable or buggy functionality some of these updates are supposed to patch probably wont be used anyways. After you reboot your system, go to the system's property page (Start>Control Panel>System OR use hotkey Win.key + break) to verify that service pack 3 was installed.

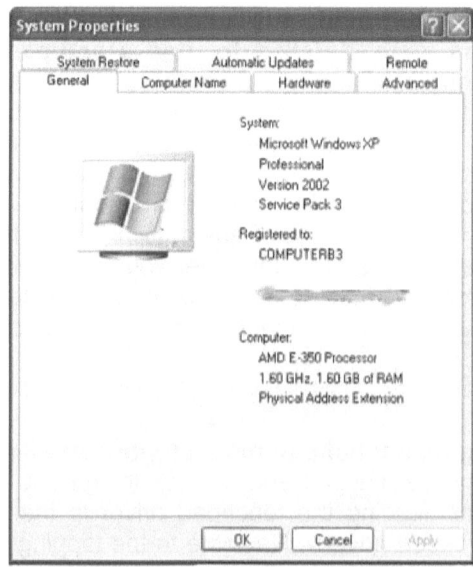
System properties tells service packs installed

18

Services
　　You may have seen these services at least once – looks like a huge list of convoluted settings that may as well have a *Do Not Touch* sign on them. Windows *services* (servers) are too often overlooked because they effect performance as much as startup programs. I can't tell you enough how much of a disservice Microsoft did for us from the start but will help correct the problem.

WARNING – Reconfiguring service, the ways described below on a Windows Vista or later can lead to adverse (and sometimes irrevocable) effects.

Configuring Services - Go to the Start menu and go into Control Panel > Administrator Tools > Services (or run *services.msc*)

　　Services are special side processes that run at startup and are conceptually kind of like daemons on Linux platforms. Services are like little servers, but for what?. A lot of services are enabled by default that you don't really need. In professional environments, a master computer with *Windows Server* is used - this is called a domain controller (DC) .
　　Windows totally has *remote access* in mind. Big organizations need better automation and network administrators to be able to go into its machines at any time. Unfortunately the features are left on by default for the home user too. You probably wont need any services that rely on domain controllers. Additionally, certain unwanted functionality can probably be turned off too like *file & printer sharing, remote desktop, NetBIOS, other sorts of things, ect.*
Configuring Log On – If your running a pre-Vista windows, all services can be set to 'Local System'. This is a very powerful setting and prevents intrusion - but it must be done to every service. Verify the change by examining the service's *Log on as* column to see that they are all set to *Local System* only. Re-sort this list if needed. If you're running anything Vista, windows 7, and up, this could in most cases **crash your system.**

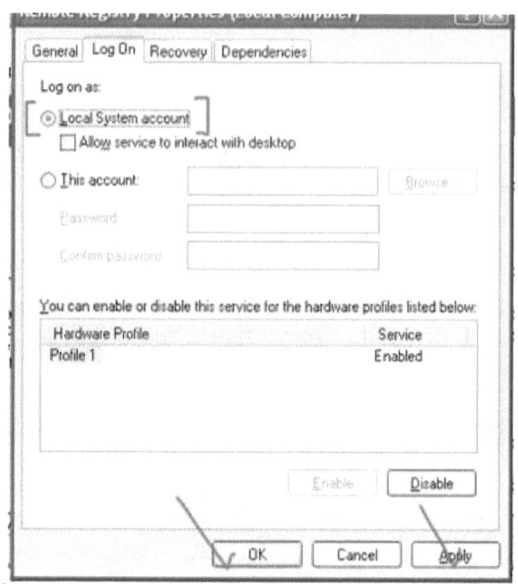

pre-vista settings for services Log On - All services should have Local System Account selected here.

You can set the state of each service in its properties page. Where it says "Startup type", select auto, manual or disabled in the dropdown form input. Don't worry about stopping any services as this is done when you reboot the computer.

A full lockdown PC is a leaner running best bet for the paranoids but there are some instances where that will limit your ability to install and use not just other Windows components but some 3rd party software. In anything Vista and later, in addition to having a lot more services, some service options listed here are greyed out.

A number of services are marked optional with ** because they are required for using network printers, remote desktop, VPN, finding local network devices or other client computers, and so on. If you opt for this kind of half-lockdown, keep in mind that Windows has other ways to disable the unwanted features a service offers.

List of services for windows xp - their default state - and their recommended state:
a=auto d=disabled m=manual
*= only used in a Windows server(domain) network.
**= required for special networking functions(VPN, RD, network printing)
bold = services not included by default

Service name	def. State	Description	Recommend
Adobe Flash Player Updater(or anything like this)	a	slows performance	Disable
Alerter*	d	Allows admins to send alerts to users in a network.	leave disabled
Application Layer Gateway Service	m		leave as is
Application Management	m		leave as is
Automatic Updates	a	Windows's obsolete automatic updates	don't want. disable this and the BITS service below.
Background Intelligent Transfer Service	m	BITS is unneeded.	disable along with automatic updates.
Bluetooth (anything)	a	**Some WLAN drivers/utilities come bundled with Bluetooth support. Disable if you dont need.**	**optional**
ClipBook	d		disabled. leave it
COM+ Event System	m	All you programmer types might know about COM libraries.	leave as is
COM+ System App.	m	COM+ related.	leave as is
Computer Browser	a	Lets Windows maintain a list of MS Clients on a network and lets you track (and be tracked).	optional
Cryptographic Services	a	important to MS's cert. management.	leave as is
DCOM Server Proc. Launcher	a		leave as is

DHCP Client	a		leave as is
Dist. Link Tracking Client	a		dont want - disable
Dist. Transaction Coordinator*	m		can be disabled
DNS Client	a		leave as is
Error Reporting Service	a	Sends error reports back to microsoft. not really needed.	disable
Event Log	a	like it says "cannot be stopped". Important to Event Viewer and logging in general.	leave as is
Extensible Authentication Protocol Service	m	Its for *Windows Clients* and wired autoconfig depends on it - somehow it looked like dead weight to me but might be better off left alone.	leave as is
Fast User Switching Compatibility	m		leave as is
Health Key and Cert Management	m	Used by Network Access Protection Agent.	Optional
Help and Support	a	Besides windows help really stinks anyways - is also known to be exploitable.	disable
HTTP SSL	m	Implements HTTPS protocol	leave as is

Human Interface Device Access	d	HID is used for among other things gaming controllers. Is disabled in SP2 but Is set to enabled by default with update.	Leave or set to automatic
IIS Admin	a	**Internet Information Service is Microsoft's web server. Not installed by default but if you have it running use caution.**	**Disable if not needed**
IMAPI CD-Burning	m	Built-in CD burning API	leave as is
Indexing Service	m	Maps your file system for remote admins.	disable here or in root folder properties.
IPSEC Services	a	Its important.	leave as is
IPv6 Helper Service	a	**Microsoft's IPv6 support.**	**optional but can do without it.**
Java Quick Starter	a	**JQS is part of Java and caused lots of undesirable CPU hogging.**	**disable**
Logical Disk Manager	a	Disk management	leave as is
Logical Disk Manager Admin.	m	Disk management	leave as is
Machine Debug manager	m	Pops in when a 3rd party disassembler is used. For **remote** software debugging(?)	you can probably disable this.
Messenger	d	An obsolete chat client.	Leave disabled
Mozilla Maintenance Service	a	**Is a updater service included with newer versions of Firefox.**	**Recommend disabling**
MS Software Shadow Copy Provider	m	Besides concurrent backups, Shadow Copy allows sneak access to filesystem.	Can be disabled along with *volume shadow copy* with no adverse effects.

Net Logon*	m	Logon authentication in Microsoft domains.	disable this
NetMeeting Remote Desktop Sharing	m	NetMeeting is a old corporate environment desktop sharing feature. Updates make this go away as well.	disable
Network Access Protection Agent	m	NAP is for a sort of self-policing or enforcement. Not totally critical.	Disable to not participate in
Network Connections	m	Your network connection objects	leave as is
Network DDE	d	DDE and network shares are something you don't want	leave disabled
Network DDE DSDM	d	see above	leave disabled
Network Location Awareness	m		leave as is
Network Provisioning Service*	m	This service is not necessary if you are a home user.	disable this
NT LM Security Support Provider	m		leave as is
Performance Logs and Alerts	m	Has to do with the performance graphs in control panel > admin tools	leave as is
Plug and Play	a	needed for Plug and Play and causes real-time detection of USB and other devices being connected or unplugged.	leave as is
Portable Media Serial # service	m	All works fine without this service.	disable

Print Spooler	a	Printer related - loads files in queue memory for later printing.	leave as is
Protected Storage	a	They say it prevents access to sensitive data.	leave as is
QoS RSVP	m	Quality of Service is supposed to improve TCP/IP packet handling somehow. This service is not required.	Optional
Remote Access Auto Connection Manager	m	Unneeded in most cases.	Disable this
Remote Access Connection Manager	m	unneeded but for windows networking / VPN client to work.	Optional**
Remote Desktop Help Session Manager	m	Remote desktop's help is said to be exploitable.	disable this
Remote Packet Capture Protocol v.0(experimental)	m	don't want	disable this
Remote Procedure Call	a	The is the one service that cannot be disabled without wrecking your system.	Just leave it alone!
Remote Procedure Call Locator	m	RPC you need but not this.	disable
Remote Registry	a	Allows remote users to modify registry settings on your computer.	disable this!
Removable Storage	m		leave as is
Routing and Remote Access	d	Helps supports VPN otherwise not needed.	Optional** (should be left disabled in most cases)

Secondary Logon	a	Lets you run things as different user.	leave as is
Security Accts. Manager	a		leave as is
Security Center	a	The too user friendly antivirus checker. It wont effect performance as it is.	leave as is
Server	a	Could be disabled for a more extreme lockdown but almost a must for administrating your own PC.	Leave as is
Shell Hardware Detection	a	More than likely needed for plug and play to work.	leave as is
Smart Card	m	Manages access to smart cards read by your computer.	Optional
SSDP Discovery Service	m	Part of Universal PNP. Needed for plug 'n play peripherals connected to LAN. The 2 services together can be disabled but sometimes are required.	Optional
System Event Notification	a	COM+ related	Leave as is
System Restore Service	a	System restore is sometimes handy for undoing messes.	Leave as is
Task Scheduler	a	Task Scheduler is essentially required for any timed events in windows.	Leave as is

TCP/IP NetBIOS Helper	a	Is really, for the most part NetBIOS Server.	Optional but recommended that both NetBIOS client and server be turned off(see *Workstation*)
Telephony	m	For networking over a telephone line with modem.	leave as is
Telnet	d	Telnet is the old terminal way of networking but this feature lets hackers try to guess your default password and get into your computer.	disable or leave disabled
Terminal Service	m	Disable if you don't need to use Remote Desktop.	Optional**
Themes	a	Windows themes	leave as is
Uninterruptible Power Supply	m	UPS are computer-connected, all-in-one battery backup +inverter.	Optional. Disable in most cases.
Universal Plug and Play	M	makes plug and play network accessible. If opting for super-lockdown, also disable SSDP service.	This and the SSDP discovery service are optional
Volume Shadow Copy	m	Allows sneak mass copy of files.	disable
Webclient	a	WebDAV related. i guess you can leave it.	Optional
Windows Audio	a	Needed for sound.	leave as is
Windows Driver Foundation	**a**	**Disabling it doesn't hurt in most cases.**	**optional**
Windows Firewall /Connection Sharing	a		leave as is

Windows Image Acquisition	m	For reading cameras/scanners.	leave as is
Windows installer	m	Needed	Leave as is
Windows Management Instrumentation	a		Leave as is
Windows Management Instrumentation Driver Extensions	m		Leave as is
Windows Media Player Network Sharing Service	a	...	**Disable**
Windows Time	a	Network time synchronization	Leave as is or optional.
Wired AutoConfig	m	networking related and a must have.	Leave as is
Wireless Zero Configuration	a	Window's built-in wifi support. leave as is unless using a 3rd party WLAN client.	Optional
WMI Performance Adapter	m	Is only Windows Media realated.	Optional
Workstation	a	Is really NetBIOS client. This service exposes your MS client info unless you disable it or NetBIOS over TCP/IP.	Optional**
World Wide Web Publishing	a	**If present, both this and IIS work together. Disable both if not required.**	**Disable**

be aware of 3rd party auto updater services and the like. Don't be afraid to disable them if needed (services and startup programs are a major cause of slowdowns). See if the software in question provides options for turning off unwanted features. For example, If you have the whole Java runtime environment installed but don't use it much anyways except for the browser plug-in, remove Java Startups and Services. Java Quick Starter (JQS) causes a lot of disc activity. At least change the settings if it lets you. Check Task Manager and you'll see jqs.exe(java Quick Starter), jucheck.exe, or jusched.exe running.

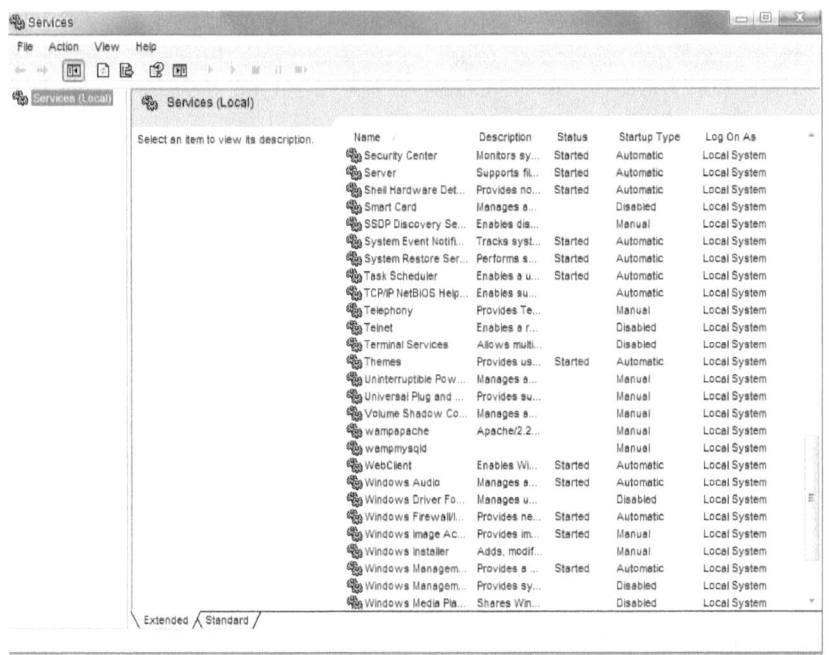

Windows XP services after configuring

Services you do need - There will be instances when Windows, and some 3rd party software, expect a service to be running in the system and fail if they are not there or disabled (this is all too true with the newer Windows). Each service properties has a *Dependencies* tab. That tells you if something depends on this service running. With a little deductive reasoning and some trial & error you should be able to spot services that are absolutely needed and which ones are dead weight. Here is a little troubleshooting guide:

Software fails to install - Some driver or software installations require Universal plug N play. Return *SSDP Discovery* and *U-PNP* services to their default auto state. Not having *Windows Installer* service running can cause installation problems too.

Printer Sharing - Its sometimes nice to have network printers at your home or office. you will need to have at the minimum NetBIOS enabled in TCP/IP advanced settings. Then *File and Printer Sharing* and *Client for MS Networks* enabled. Leave *Workstation* service running. You might also need *TCP/IP NetBIOS helper* running if you're serving a network printer.

29

NOTE: - Occasionally recheck and verify the service's startup and running states. A unintended change here could indicate something you installed earlier tampered with them.

Disabling Startup Programs Using MS Configuration Utility

Startup programs can be set up unknowingly to the average user. There is a built-in tool for making changes to these entries. From admin account, go to MS configuration utility. Click start > run, type msconfig.exe. Unlike other windows tools, msconfig is actually located in:

c:\WINDOWS\pchealth\helpctr\binaries\msconfig.exe

From here you can boot with or without config.sys, autoexec.bat or any other startup items. The *Startup* tab is of most importance. Uncheck any startup programs you don't need. if you're unsure what startups go to what software, don't worry. Its usually safe to disable everything if needed. Most big name software will have their startup entries here but the *startup* folder in your **start menu** sometimes has them too. Additionally, The *services* tab lets you completely remove windows built-in or 3rd party services. Sometimes its really clear when something needs to be removed but services are better to adjust in the *services.msc* template.

Turning Off Autoplay

Autoplay is a annoying feature that windows forced on its users a long time ago. It causes software from USB drives and discs to be ran without you having much to say about it. Some malware even count on this just to install their payload. Autoplay looks for a autorun.inf file on the newly mounted volume and runs the commands therein. There are a few different ways to turn off autoplay. You will want to disable autoplay system-wide or on each user account(including admin). Reboot for change to take effect.

- **Powertoys Tweak UI** - Tweak UI is one of many unofficial software tools available through the MS website. it lets you among other things, completely disable autoplay(but not in the same way that gpedit does). Doing it this way, you have to use Tweak UI to disable autoplay on **each user account**. (while promoted to admin)in the left pane tree view go into my computer>autoplay and uncheck all the drives then under Types, uncheck anything to do with autoplay, click Apply or OK when done.
- **Group Policy Editor** - With gpedit.msc you can disable autoplay. This change is supposed to be system-wide and autoplay should get disabled for all users.
  - Click Start, click Run, type gpedit.msc in the Open box, and then click OK.

- Under Computer Configuration, expand Administrative Templates, and then click System.
- In the Settings pane, right-click Turn off Autoplay, and then click Properties.
- Click Enabled, and then select All drives in the Turn off Autoplay box to disable Autorun on all drives.
- Click OK to close the Turn off Autoplay Properties dialog box.
- Restart the computer.

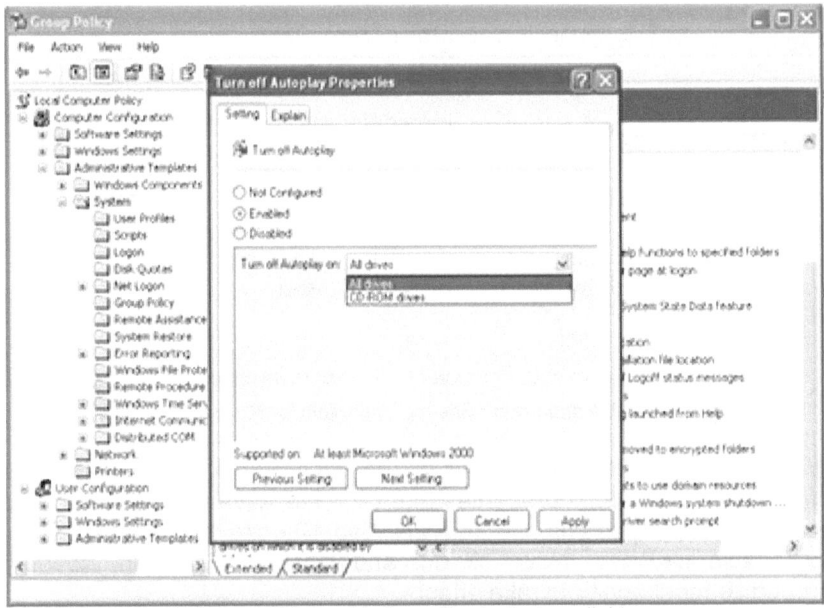

Using gpedit to enable 'turn off autoplay' on all drives.

- Disabling Autoplay in Registry Editor? - There is a sure way to alter registry keys and disable autoplay but i'm not delving into this here since the other ways work just fine.

Network Connections

The network connections properties is where you find all the windows settings, and right down to the driver for a network connection (such as modem, NIC card, WLAN). The components windows sticks you with by default allow you to be hacked and need adjustment (even though we turned services for these off earlier). Windows groups its network components as *client, service,* or *protocol.* You can install additional components like for IPv6 protocol, Novell Netware, and so on.

From your admin acct. go to S*tart>Control Panel>Network Connections* or double click the networking icon in the notification area on the bottom right. In the list below where it says *This connection uses the following items,* you only really need the ***Internet Protocol TCP/IP*** item. everything else can go and it'll still work. Uncheck *File and printer sharing* and **Client For MS Networks** since your probably not using these. You could also uncheck anything else if you like: *QoS, AEGIS protocol,* and *link-layer topology responder.*

This connection uses the following items:

- [ ] Client for Microsoft Networks
- [ ] VirtualBox Bridged Networking Driver
- [ ] File and Printer Sharing for Microsoft Networks
- [✔] QoS Packet Scheduler

[Install...] [Uninstall] [Properti...]

Description
Allows your computer to access resources on a Microsoft

Keep items 'File and Printer Sharing' and Client for MS Networks disabled.

WINS and NetBIOS - To be doubly sure MS's built-in exploitability is turned off, go into the TCP/IP properties and click the Advanced settings. Another properties sheet pops up. On the WINS tab, Choose the bottom radio button to Disable netBIOS. Now, ok out and close the Network connections properties for changes to take effect.

- Repeat these steps for all connection objects. This may only be your NIC or additionally your WLAN as well.

NOTE: When you install components or make similar changes on network settings, you might have to again uncheck the unwanted components.

System Properties(optional) - Its in Control Panel but pressing WIN+Break or running 'sysdm.cpl' also takes you to system properties. Under **Computer Name**, the computer name can be edited. This name is used to form your DNS and is what networks identify you by along with your MAC. Under **Automatic Updates** leave Automatic Updates alone as trying to disable it may cause nag popups. On the **Remote** tab, it doesn't hurt to be sure Remote Desktop and Remote Assistant are unchecked (even though we probably already turned those off earlier).

While you're here, look at the General and Computer Name tabs to look at processor type, speed and to verify your name and computer name were set and to see that SP3 was installed.

Adjusting Power Options - These settings are important and can save you from wondering why your computer goes to sleep when you don't want it to. As administrator privilege only, Go to Start > Control Panel > Power Settings or run 'powercfg.cpl'. Here you can adjust how many minutes your screen and computer stay on after not in use, program power and sleep buttons, and enable hibernation, the better sleep.

Tweaking Event Viewer Settings(optional) - Event viewer logs the going-ons of windows. To increase and improve event logs, open Start>Control Panel>Administrative Tools>Event Viewer or run 'eventvwr.exe'. On the left side pane, open the properties on Application, Security, and System. Do this to all items. Set the max log size to something much bigger and select 'overwrite as needed'. Click OK.

Adding/removing groups in any user account(optional) - Should you ever think you may need higher than admin access to your own computer, open Start>Control Panel>Administrative Tools>Computer Management. On the left side pane, expand local users and groups then click Users.

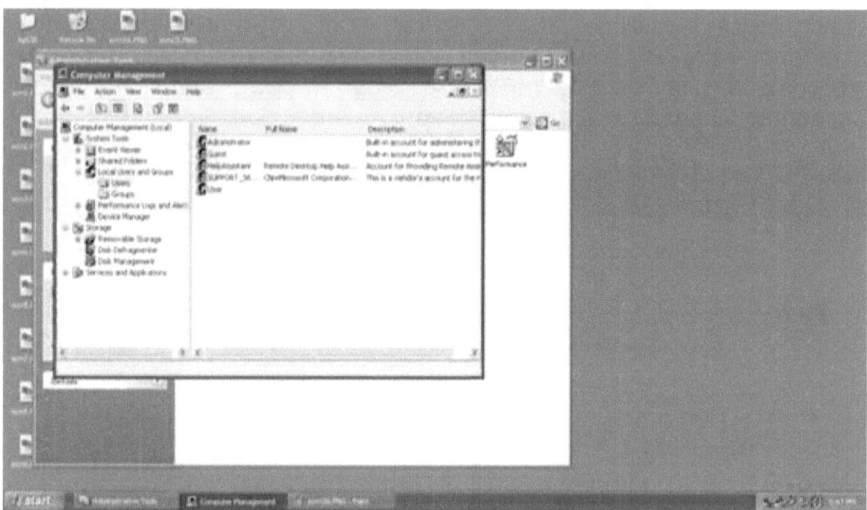

Double click Administrator then on the Member Of tab, click 'Add'. Another window pops up to let you add more groups. Click 'Advance...'

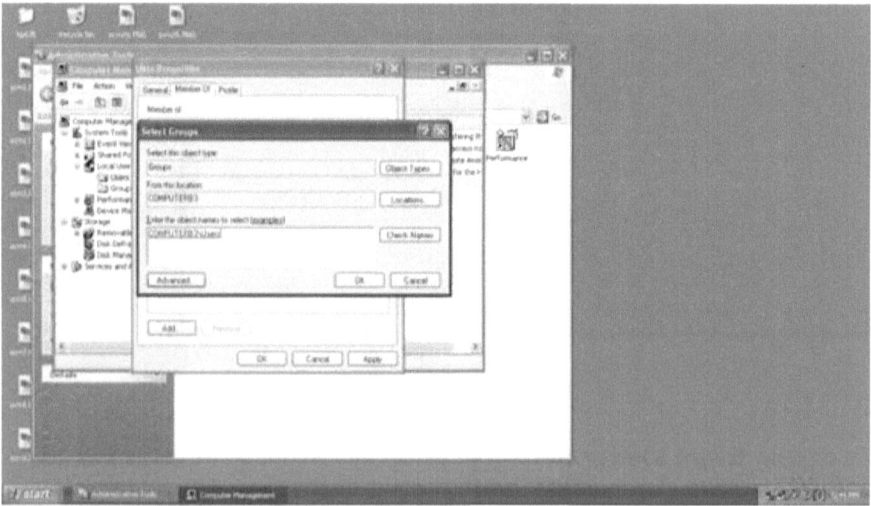

Another window pops up, click 'Find now' with no criteria and all the default and built-in groups get listed below. Select the group(s) you want.

Now you should have 1 or more groups in the properties page. Selecting too many groups (maybe in the wrong order) causes access problems, like with using event viewer. Click Apply or OK to complete setting.

Never remove your single admin account from Administrators group since this could lock you out of your computer! Make sure your Admin/Administrator acct. is a member of the Administrators group and your lower privileged accounts are only a member of the Users or Guest group.

lower privileges on user account(s) - Once you turned off autoplay and adjusted the power settings in your user acct., you can remove it from the administrators group. This makes your user account much less exploitable or risky to use. You can also create more user accounts if you like.

Demote your user account by going to control panel>user accounts, and then your already created account name. Change account type. It should let you switch from administrators to limited user. If you are using regular Home edition Windows, this is the only place you can do it. Sometimes the limited user is greyed out and might need to reboot in Safe Mode to change this. Otherwise go to Computer Management under Admin Tools in Control Panel or run 'compmgmt.msc'. Select Users node in left pane, go to your user account that you named earlier on the user's properties, go to the 'Member of' tab and remove 'Administrators' group. You should only have 'Users' group here now. click ok.

Managing things from a non admin acct - First, make a shortcut to 'cmd.exe' on your desktop. Its located in c:\windows\system32. Use the 'run as...' menu option in the right click menu and with the shortcut you just made, open a command line window as administrator. From here you can run commands as administrator while in a lower privilege account.

Your almost done - Check performance in Task Manager - Type control + left shift + escape to open Task Manager. It should stay around 0% processor usage when its sitting idle. Additionally, dual core processors should show up with 2 CPU usage graphs.

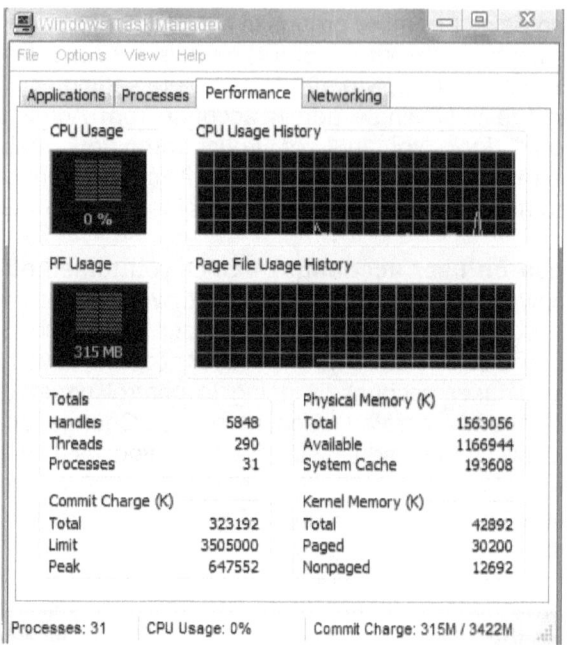

Only a few things should really gobble up performance. File manipulation, opening files, the OS performs housekeeping during screensaver time, and web browsing or video games to name some. If everything looks right, you can connect computer online.

Firewalls - A firewall can block unwanted access to your computer. Firewalls can be a software program or a physical unit at the front of your home network. **A stand-alone firewall unit -** Suppose your in a business environment and must have printer sharing, NetBIOS and whatever else. This is where a network firewall is needed to protect your workstations from intrusion, thereby limiting the risky functionality to only your local network. Block known proprietary MS features, filter by port #, packet structure, and whatever else. Unless high speed is a concern, older units might be only 10Mbps but still work adequately in many cases. Firewalls have ethernet jacks on the back and can be physically added as a gateway between your private intranet LAN and the online cable modem. Software firewalls intercept network traffic in your computer and run in the background (but should never effect performance). Windows already has 2-way port/IP blocking capability but we'll get into that in a later chapter.

Windows firewall - A predictable inbound blocking firewall.
- Go into Windows Firewall. type firewall.cpl on command line or go to Start>Control Panel>Security Center>Windows Firewall
- On the exceptions tab, uncheck everything. (checking 'dont allow exceptions' on the general tab should have same effect.)

-- In Chapter 6 i'll show you how to firewall Windows with IPSec

36

Optional cosmetic touch - A Windows 7 Theme?

To open Display Properties right click almost anywhere on the desktop, Go to Properties an then select the themes tab. This is where you load and save themes. a '.theme' file itself is just a config or resource locater text file. you need images and other files that go along with. Do a little web surfing and you could find many already made up themes+resources.

In some cases, there are several themes already provided, select a different theme in the drop-down list.

Creating or installing themes is a not too hard thing. I seen a good article on how to do this, somewhere. Everything in windows is customizable including the icon sizes, fonts, cursors, and those tell-tale XP default .wav sounds (played during startup and shutdown, and error sounds)

Themes are under c:\windows\resources. The windows 7 blue theme is a little incomplete but some of the newfangled icons and cursors are under a different theme for some reason. After 20 minutes of tweaking, this would fool just about anyone!

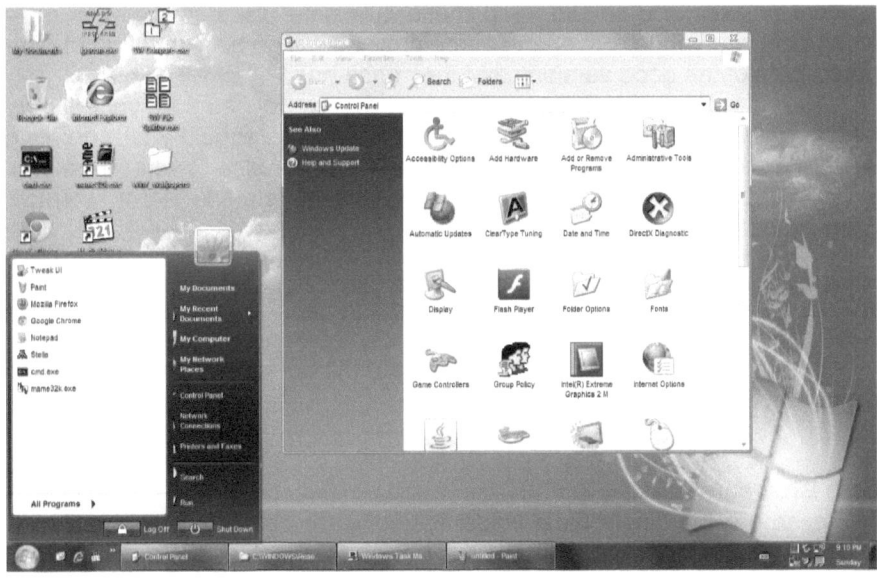

...Always down with the latest bro.

...and that's all. You now have a much more secure computer than it was *out of box*!

Chapter 3 - 3rd Party Software

This is any software that didn't come with Windows. Some examples are the computer software bought at the store, free trial or open source Windows compatible software available for download, or any supplemental software that came with other products. 3rd party software can be on a Distribution CD disc or in a 1 file(or more) self extracting *installer*. Some commercial software on disc was made to *autoplay* but with autoplay turned off, you just have to navigate to the cd drive and run the main setup file, usually called something like 'setup.msi' or.exe and open that. The installer is ran one time and the software can then be used.

Using software you downloaded from somewhere and then running/installing it as admin is risky, to say the least. Any software should be researched. What do others say about it? Whats the credibility of the place you got it from? Does it look too good to be true? If possible, test the software on a junker computer or *virtual machine* to see what it does first. Watch it in task manager. Does it have too much going on and slow down everything? Does it have to connect online? Its better to be safe than to have a messed up Windows, You may think this is nuts but I tend to favor the earlier and most stable beta releases of a free/open source software product. In fact, you should keep these in a safe place. You never know when software vendors or open source projects will go belly up and not offer downloads of the good versions that they once had.

Service Packs/Updates - These are nice to keep in your library because you want to be able to reapply the updates should your operating system go to hell. So you should save them installer files or what have you. Windows service packs are important when starting from scratch. Sometimes you need these on hand:

WindowsXP-KB835935-SP2-ENU.exe (278,927,592bytes) - Service Pack 2
WindowsXP-KB936929-SP3-x86-ENU.exe (331,805,736bytes) - Service Pack 3

Any other updates or SPs should be able to be kept in your new offline files collection.

Web Browsers
These are the single most influential software products ever. Every PC and Mac instantly went from being geeky forgettables to a full-fledged corporate marketing tool because of the converging of text, images, and streaming audio/video, in a clean newspaper like way. These web surfing tools combine various software technologies, in a modular fashion, into a single app - and web browsers are also a big cause of computer vulnerability. If any of the browser's side programs can signal a glitch to crash the system or worse, write, modify, or delete a critical system file then your computer is in jeopardy anytime you visit the wrong website.

The following are good web browsers:

Old Firefox V1,2, or 3 - FREE - Being phased out for sure but usually still works much of the time. Never mind those online gimmicks saying your everything is out of date. Linux distributions come with even a more outdated firefox version than this.

Internet Explorer 6 - Great for downloading a better browser.

New Firefox - FREE - Newer versions, like version 4 and beyond. work as advertised but looking more like the competitors than earlier versions. Advertiser tracking opt-in/out options, the latest HTML5 support, and other user friendly features included.

Google Chrome - COMMERCIAL/FREE - Fresh look. Handles newest standards and then some. Tons of free apps & extensions to try out but Chrome comes with some security holes too. Disable Flash.

PDF software:

these are good alternatives to Acrobat Reader:

FoxitReader v3.1.1.0901(5,303,552bytes) - SHAREWARE - Alternative to acrobat reader. Full version available for a price.

SumatraPDF v2.5.2.0 - FREE - Another good PDF reader. Also can convert document files between various formats - allowing you to make your own PDF files.

A/V Players:

these are good alternatives instead of Windows Media Player:

VideoLAN (VLC) media player - FREE – Little confused about the LAN part of it but plays most video/audio formats, streaming video, Also, the cone icon gets a Santa cap at Christmas! VLC has excellent controls for graphic equalizer and surround sound.

Media Player Classic - FREE - Also seems to play just about anything. Has a bit of trouble playing SWF games because the arrow keys double for volume control.

Compression Software – Besides Window's built-in zip folder functionality, there is newer and better 3rd party software.

WinRAR - COMMERCIAL/FREE TO TRY - Very good

7Zip v9.20 - FREE - Very good. Supports encryption.

Network Utilities:

Angry IP Scanner v2.21(111,104bytes) - FREE - Helpful program for do-it-yourselfers - finds ip hosts in your network.

Wireshark v1.2.5 (18,337,408bytes) - FREE - The best program for packet sniffing.

lvllord TCP/IP patch - FREE - This removes the 10 concurrent connection limit.

Text editors:

Crimson editor v3.70(1,253,038bytes) – FREE – Excellent text editor for multiple programming languages and color codes commands and expressions. Handles Linux and Mac text files but chokes on large text files lacking in end-of-line characters.

Notepad – BUILT-IN – Still a good simple text editor.

Word Processor/Spreadsheet/Presentation

Microsoft Office 2000, XP - COMMERCIAL - popular product for PC's because newer versions stink.

Open Office - FREE - Replacement for MS Office. It works but takes lots of getting used to.

ISO Imaging / Burning

ISO Imaging Allows creating a sector-by-sector disk image of almost any drive, and then comes out as a single, compressed file.

ISOrecorder v2.0(369,152bytes) - FREE - Allows you to burn bootable ISO CD discs. no problems.

nLite v1.4.9.1(2,665,796bytes) - FREE - Software that lets you make changes to the Windows installation CD and make bootable copies.

Nero Burning ROM - COMMERSIAL - Good product.

MagicISO – FREE TO TRY – Excellent user interface. Burns bootable ISOs, editable metadata, many options.

Encryption – Cryptography is really a bid deal these days. More and more everything gets encrypted. There is encrypted information, communication, bank transactions, and even entire currencies like *Bitcoin*. Truth is any amateur programmer could concoct their own unbreakable encryption scheme, its almost as easy as the old codebreaker puzzles. Yet the encryption standards that are widely used presently are *public key/private key* encryption, with snazzy algorithms like AES, and others. Only the private key can decipher a message. The public key is given away to receive encrypted messages only. Security here relies on large enough keys that make it as unbreakable as needed. *Certificates* and *CA*'s play into this too as they're supposed to reassure that certificate holders are who they say they are.

WinRAR and **7Zip** – FREE TO TRY - Archiving software. Already has a password encryption ability.

PGP – FREE TO TRY - I heard the founder of Pretty Good Privacy went out of business years ago. Is now a Symantec product so, the untouched, original PGP is probably what you really want. Older is better.

GPG – OPEN SOURCE – GnuPGP project. A newer and improved PGP.

OpenVPN - FREE

Paid Encryption software packages, Stegenos, maybe others, etc – allow much bigger public/private keys. Better hands down.

Rootkit/Virus scanners:

NoAdware - COMMERCIAL - A underrated virus scanner that's been around awhile. Just scan system files, registry, and known spyware locations then exit out. Will always find new stuff after web surfing as admin.

Hijack this! - FREE –

Rootkit Revealer - FREE - not really a removal tool but can find if a hacker planted their tools-of-the-trade on you.

Luke Filewalker - FREE - Might be ok.

Malwarebytes - COMMERCIAL/FREE - If you just have to use something that looks like a anti-virus suite, this one worked ok.

...And there is more good ones out there, somewhere.

"Antivirus" and other similar products:

I won't name the product. They claim their software is like a piece of bad medicine every computer must take. The things spit out annoying pop-ups nagging you to do trivial things that have nothing to do with keeping you safe. Besides making your computer slow(and permanently crippled), these types of software can allow themselves to take over your whole computer, and do who knows what with it - read the contract. If you simply don't make mistakes like opening (which invokes run) unknown files with '.exe' at the end, letting yourself get hacked first so you actually need daily scans, and so on, then you would never need this kind of software in your computer.

Simply avoid this gimmick with a passion!

Virtual Machines:

Like popular video game emulators, virtualization was a, pardon the pun, big game changer. They allow you to run a semi-emulated PC within software thereby sandboxing the entire operating system in case something goes wrong. Also they allow you to run as many VM's as you like, even at the same time if your computer can handle it. Some even allow easy remote access, just like a remote desktop session. Server hosting firms use virtualized space for their clients, which eliminates risk of server downtime. Virtualization takes some processing overhead so a operating system running virtually may run about 70% the speed as it would running on the native hardware. VirtualBox and VMWare both let you install a virtual NIC card, move files in and out of your virtual machine or with USB drive.

42

One good use for virtual machining is to set up a junkable Windows VM. Abuse this in any way while the base operating system never gets effected. Testbed questionable software packages or even trojan horse malware, see what these things do and take screen shots.

The most popular VM software products are:

VMWare - COMMERCIAL - Very good!

VirtualBox v2.2.4 (66,026,000bytes) - FREE(to try) - Very good! I think its still free.

Virtual PC - COMMERCIAL - Works. Microsoft's own answer to VM'ing. Older versions are really slow.

Remote Access:
Imagine being out of town and yet able to log into your computer at home to, open up files, configure settings, respond to email, check webcams and microphones. These kind of tools allow you to do that.

TeamViewer - Free - Alternative to Remote Desktop. Allows you to log in and control other TeamViewer computers remotely.

Skype – COMMERCIAL/PAY AS YOU GO – Phone & video chat. It started out as a free product but might take too many liberties on your system now, if you know what I mean.

Remote Desktop - The plain old built-in original works fine. Can even still be secure with some minor security tweaks.

Chapter 4 - Management and System Maintenance Tips

Now that you set up your computer from scratch minus all the non-essentials, configured settings, and loaded in some useful software, you now should learn your way around windows using command line and all its tools.

Create a cmd.exe shortcut - Log on to your limited user account. Right-click somewhere on desktop and choose New > Shortcut, and the create Shortcut wizard pops up. either click browse... to select the windgows\system32 directory or just type C:\WINDOWS\system32\cmd.exe. Click Next. The name provided should be good enough so click Finish and you now should have a icon for opening command line on your desktop.

Use Run As... - Too many settings cannot be changed without higher access and others will do more. Sometimes you actually have to stop what you're doing and switch users to make changes but usually not. Right click the cmd.exe shortcut and select run as...(Windows Vista and up has *Run as Administrator* instead...ugg). Select the radio button next to 'the following user' and select the Administrator or Admin in the drop-down list and enter the password. Click Ok. Command line window pops up.

Basic MS-DOS

Not Case Sensitive – MS-DOS commands can be typed in upper or lower case.

No need to type .exe – All commands end with *.exe* and MS-DOS assumes this for you.

Where are commands located – Most the actual commands are located in C:\WINDOWS\system32. No matter what folder you're into on command, MS-DOS/Windows uses environmental variables that setup system32 as a default folder to run executables from.

Drive Letters - First of all, all your devices that can get mapped into the file system, whether its the hard disk, floppy, flash drives, SD cards, optical drives, many other USB devices, maybe even tape backup, Microsoft designates them with a drive letter.

A: B: C: D: ... Z:

Drives are lettered a-z (or A-Z). This is also the beginning part of a fully qualified pathname.

NTFS vs. FAT32 – FAT is the internal file system used back in earlier days. Windows still talks to FAT32 file system and still formats detachable storage as such.

dir - the file directory command
  Syntax: dir {file name and/or wildcards} [/w][/p][/a][/s]
example:
```
dir
```
lists files in current directory/folder.

Or,

```
cd c:\
dir *.* /a/s/w
```
 lists all the files on your entire hard drive.

cd - change Directory command
Syntax: cd <directory name>example:
Examples:

```
cd thisdir
```
Go into subdirectory 'thisdir'

```
cd..
```
Go back a directory

```
cd\
```
Go into root

Many more basic commands like md, copy, xcopy, move, format, deltree, attrib, rename, del, and others – GET A REFERENCE MANUAL

runas - Run as another user. Same as it's GUI counterpart. Good for running a program under another user account credentials (such as Admin)

Syntax:

  runas [/noprofile /env] /user:<computer name>\<user> <command>

OR
  runas [/noprofile /env] /user:<user>@<computer name> <command>

optional switches: /noprofile /env - using both may cause runas to take up less overhead.

Run MS Configuration Utility as admin example:

```
runas /noprofile /env /user:COMPUTERB3\Admin
c:\WINDOWS\pchealth\helpctr\binaries\msconfig.exe
```

assoc - File associations, that is, which 3 or more letter .ext or file type opens which software. 'assoc' allows you to change a file association too. these are the same settings as whats in *Explorer > Tools > Folder Options > File Types tab*

Syntax: assoc [<.ext>[=[<FileType>]]]

example:
```
assoc
```
displays all file associations in Windows.

driverquery - display list of drivers

example:
```
driverquery -v
```
displays more info

tasklist - List running tasks
examples:

```
tasklist
```
Lists all running tasks

```
tasklist -svc
```
Shows services.

```
tasklist -v
```
Tasks with more information.

```
tasklist -m
```
Locates .dll's associated with tasks.

GUI Tools:

Task Manager – taskmgr.exe - Use command line or go to Start>Run… and type taskmgr.exe (the hotkey is shift+ctrl+esc). Shows details about running processes and applications. You can also stop or start processes in task manager. Also lets you monitor computer performance and a lot of other things. Programmers can use it to spot memory leaks in their own apps. It might be of benefit to run this as admin as stopping some processes could give you a 'access denied' if you dont have sufficient privilege.

MS Configuration Manager – msconfig.exe - Configures startup files, services, tools, and lets you adjust startup mode and customize the old windows .INI files. On the startup and services tab you select which applications and services get loaded automatically. Many 3rd party softwares will add themselves to these lists. A major cause of slow down is from having too many startup programs. As admin Go to Start>Run... and type msconfig.exe or on command line type:

```
c:\WINDOWS\pchealth\helpctr\binaries\msconfig.exe
```

Command Line (MS-DOS mode) - cmd.exe - This is the traditional prompt within Windows. Go to Start > Run... and type 'cmd' or 'cmd.exe' and hit enter. Almost anything the GUI has can be called from command line. The GUI shortcuts are listed in the appendix section. Some useful commands will be supplied along the way. I can't stress enough that you should know the basics about MSDOS and command line.

Microsoft Management Console - mmc.exe - The Shang Tsung of admin tools. Think of this as a administrator tools construction set. MMC is at the root of all the control panel's .msc files, also known as MMC templates. Run this and go to File > 'add/remove snap-in'. Click 'Add...' and you'll see a list of everything and then some like computer management, event viewer, device manager, services, gpedit, and all that other stuff. Click Add 1 time for each item you want to manage. Some snap-ins ask if you want to use for remote or local computer. Leave as local computer then Ok. Close when done adding and click Ok. All the snap-ins appear on the navigation pane on the left. Just like regedit, the changes made to settings take effect immediately or after you reboot. When you close MMC it asks you if you want to save. This only saves the customized .msc console template that you created by adding snap-ins. So you're fine to click 'No' and close the window when finished. So templates with any combo of snap-ins give many other possibilities besides just the default Control Panel's Administrator Tools.

Registry Editors - regedit.exe, regedt32.exe - Historically speaking, probably the first management console. The registry is Microsoft's answer to centralizing configuration settings. Developers use the registry instead of config files. Any Windows setting can be found in this enormous data directory structure. Think of registry editor as a low-level admin tool. You can also import and export registry changes as text files with a .reg extension. Use with caution. The safer Regedt32 doesn't immediately make the changes until you close out.

Local Security Settings

Go to *Start* then *Run...* type *gpedit.msc*. These kind of settings are sometimes called *policies*, as if to emphasize the security nature of Windows NT. The gpedit template sits nearer to the top of the pyrimid then many others. The settings here are as follows:

> **Startup/shutdown Scripts** – Allowing scripts to run. Nothing here by default.

> **Account policies** – your lockdown counter, should somebody attempt to brute force your computer's password.

> **Local policies** – Contains *Auditing, User Rights assignment, and Security Options.* I will delve into auditing further on. The other 2 contain many various little adjustments that can effect how you logon or what *group* can do what actions, that trickles down to user account privileges. for example, you set things so members of the Users group can change the system time(normally only Admins and Power Users groups can do this). That way your lowly User account can more easily see or even set the time.

> **Public Key Policies** – encryption stuff.

> **Software Restriction**

> **IP Security Policies** – IPSec helps you configure a firewall.

> **Administrative Templates** – Many various, even redundant settings

> **User Configuration** – Many various, even redundant settings.

48

File Management Basics

Copying vs. moving NTFS files - You may already realize the difference between copying and moving but let me go over this using the GUI method as example. When you drag and drop a file or folder to another folder or your desktop, without holding control, you are only moving a file. Copying a file is when you not relocate the source file but make a copy of it. You do so by dragging and dropping while holding down the Control key. Now imagine you are logged in as full admin and you need to give a lower priv. user a file. the file itself may contain security settings that only allow you the admin to ever read or even see it. If you just move this into the limited user's desktop, they may not ever be able to read that file, much less change or delete it, but get a *access denied*. How do you give this file to this user? Simple, you copy it. That's right. You can't move it but the copy of that file will inherit the security permissions of the parent folder you're copying it to. The rules change when you move a file from/to a different volume, that is like, for example your flash drive. The OS has it worked out that it automatically becomes a copy operation and the source file should not be changed or moved.

Doing backups - Save your work - Any pro knows to make backups of their clients or their own work. When doing a backup, you don't need to save every file on the hard drive. You only need to save things like your own data files, especially ones you change periodically. Perhaps there are interesting things you downloaded that should be saved? If you have various document files scattered throughout your computer – who know where – That's real sloppy! Browse your file system till you find out where each and every one of them is located, make copies and if possible relocate where the software saves your files. Copying files in and out of your Windows computer is simple drag and drop stuff. Copy/move entire folders at a time - no problem! Get acquainted with the entire directory structure and where everything is located. For example, the files in a users desktop are located in the folder c:\documents and settings\User\Desktop. All the installed programs are located in c:\Program Files but these should almost never be backed up - only the installer file(s) or the software CD/DVD is needed. Don't be a old lady! Keeping documents and other sorts of data files, no matter what software you might have opened or saved them with, **together in one location preferably,** like the User's Documents folder or even the desktop, makes things much easier later on.

Backup the following:
- **Obvious Things** - These are things of interest you created or obtained somehow. Movies, games, pictures, Those love letters from your girlfriend, personal documents, sound clips, whatever.

- **Software Installers** - If the software is not as a single executable, and it installs itself (in \program files) you need to only backup the software's all-in-one installer file(s). Disc-based software, you just need the software's disc ROM.
- **Drivers** - The drivers for your computer, additional drivers like for printers or other peripherals you use. Like most commercial products, these usually come as installer files or from the original recovery disc.
- **Program Data** - These are any data files created by software like email, favorites, bookmarks or links to websites, config files, and so on. These may be hidden in the file system. There may be times when you want to save software's configuration or certain log files. When that time comes **Don't move these files** as that might effect the current operability of the software, but copy these all together in one folder for backup.

Saving your own important files takes much less space than trying to do a full backup of your entire hard drive - However if you ever do need to entirely back up everything there are low level disc copiers, thereby getting you a **exact image** that can be restored.

Where To Save – Below is a list of possible storage options:
- Burn to discs with Rewritable CD/DVD/BluRay optical drive.
- A USB detachable memory device (thumb drive, SSD, or what have you)
- Another Hard Disk connected as slave or via an adapter.
- Upload to a NAS or another computer on your network.
- Tape backup
- Cloud storage, If this is your thing.
- Zip or floppy drive (sigh)

More File Management Basics

Adjusting access to file and folder objects - Windows with *NTFS* (New Technology File System) allows individual security settings for every file on your hard drive. As a admin your job is to delegate which users get to do what with which files. Since we are only working with something like 2 accounts, maybe more if need be later on, one being Admin, and you the reader are the only actual person using any of them, are aim is just to restrict your single non-admin user account from wrecking the system should something go wrong. That's why members of only the *Users* group can't make changes to system files and we like it this way. *Access Control Lists* tell Windows which users get to read, write, delete, modify, and so on, to a particular file or folder. Right Click a file or folder and go to its properties page. Here admins should see a *Security* tab. This is where you grant access, to Users and Groups, and specify how much. Think of this, as you'll see later on, as being your own computer policeman – and yet its all just geeky computer inner-workings underneath it all.

You may never need to know any of this except if you want to make permissions tweaks or have folders on c:\ root drive and you want to allow account *User* write or just full control of files somewhere. Adjustments to access are best to make to the built-in *Users* group rather that account *User* itself sometimes. Never Deny access to something as a rule of thumb as it just makes a big mess. Tailoring the ACL's to allow read/write, read, or no access by users, Grant or Deny, and applying settings to all subfolders & objects therein, (mass changing ACLs) can be risky, and time consuming endeavors.

Auditing – Suppose someone's compromised your computer and you want to catch them. Windows has something already built-in for that.

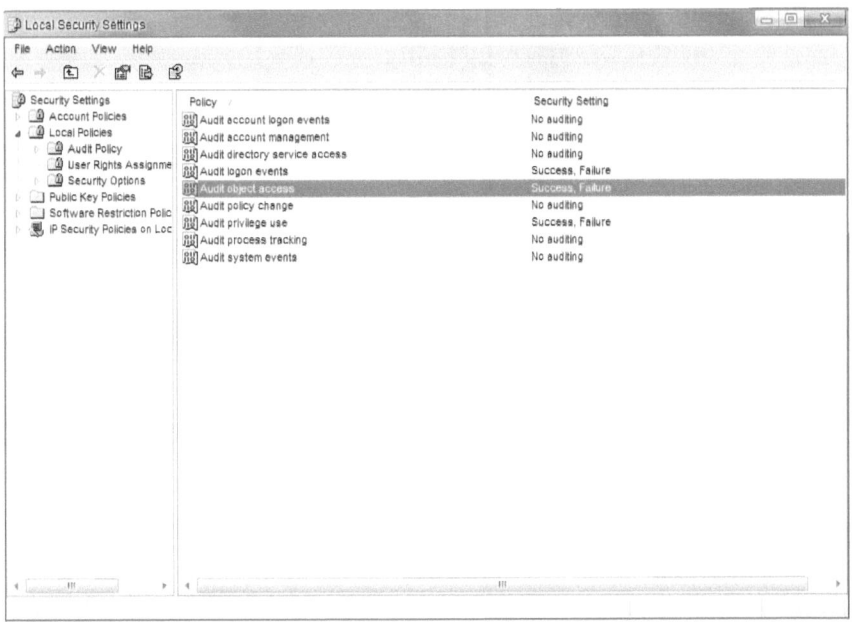

Now don't get mixed up by this jargon. Think of auditing as setting some alarm bells whenever yourself, someone else, or even the system succeeds or fails to access your computer. Expand *Local Policy* and select *Audit Policy* in the left pane. You now can enable and change the items in the right hand pane. Logon events tell whenever logins occur, and auditing object access, objects being files & folders, tell you whenever files are accessed in your computer and by which user. events will show up in relation to the auditing you enabled. Open up event viewer - *eventvwr.exe* or under *Control Panel>Admin Tools*. Expand 'Security' on the left pane. You will see here logging of all the audit events you just enabled. Along with your known user and admin accounts, you'll also see some mysterious accounts like from SYSTEM, NETWORK SERVICE, and so on, even on the NT AUTHORITY domain. these are local system events. Because all your services are set as local system, there should be no 3rd party activity.

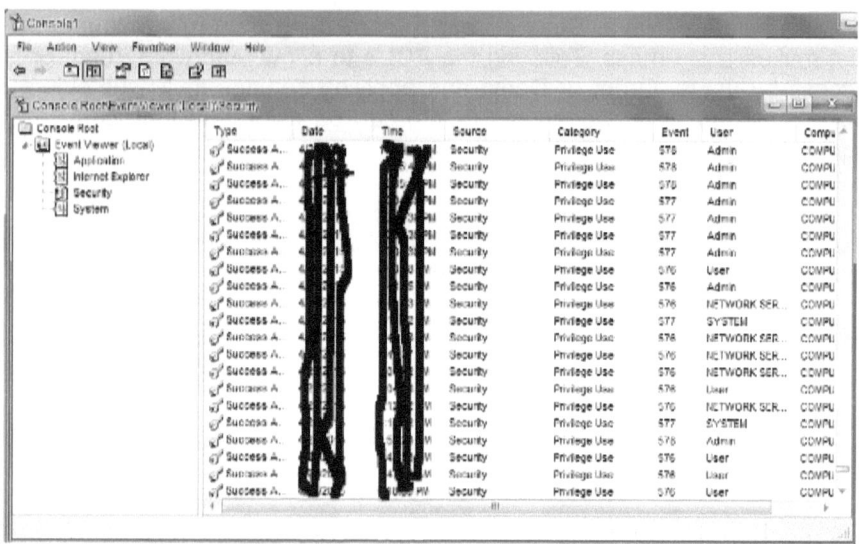

Security Audits can be lengthy. Its best to only set auditing for the fewest things possible.

Sometimes a event or audit description seems kind of vague. Event IDs can be looked up and complete lists can be found elsewhere. Below is a incomplete list of the lowest number event ID codes and their meanings:

The first (of many) event ID error codes are as follows:

Event ID code	Description
512	Windows NT is starting up
513	Windows is shutting down
514	An authentication package has been loaded by the Local Security Authority
515	A trusted logon process has registered with the Local Security Authority
516	Internal resources allocated for the queuing of audit messages have been exhausted, leading to the loss of some audits
517	The audit log was cleared
518	A notification package has been loaded by the Security Account Manager
519	A process is using an invalid local procedure call (LPC) port
520	The system time was changed

521	Unable to log events to security log
528	Successful Logon
529	Logon Failure – Unknown user name or bad password
530	Logon Failure - Account logon time restriction violation
531	Logon Failure - Account currently disabled
532	Logon Failure - The specified user account has expired
533	Logon Failure - User not allowed to logon at this computer
534	Logon Failure - The user has not been granted the requested logon type at this machine
535	Logon Failure - The specified account's password has expired
536	Logon Failure - The NetLogon component is not active
537	Logon failure - The logon attempt failed for other reasons.
538	User Logoff
539	Logon Failure - Account locked out
540	Successful Network Logon
551	User initiated logoff
552	Logon attempt using explicit credentials

Chapter 5 - Networking Crash Course

History

Back in the not so distant past, before the World Wide Web, Home computers networked through the telephone lines. The old terminal/mainframe networking model was king and they used *telnet* exclusively with terminal emulator software. Computer users with a modem were able to call up bulletin boards(BBS) or switch to half-duplex and call your friend's computer directly, send/receive text(somewhat graphical) and upload and download files, and capture text. This was free as long as you had phone service (unless you called long distance or used pay-as-you-go services like CompuServe). You could text others or leave messages, public, private, or in real time. The emotion symbols like smiley faces :) and all the jargon and online etiquettes used today got its start in the telnet days. There was something more secure-feeling about this mode of networking - was even a time you could get on the Internet with nothing but a terminal.

With advances in computer tech, along with higher data speeds, graphics, sound, and more sophisticated software, TCP/IP and the world-wide-web's client/server networking model became more widespread, the browser replaces terminal mode, and telnet is neatly put away in a box as another protocol.

Wiring example of 4-port home network

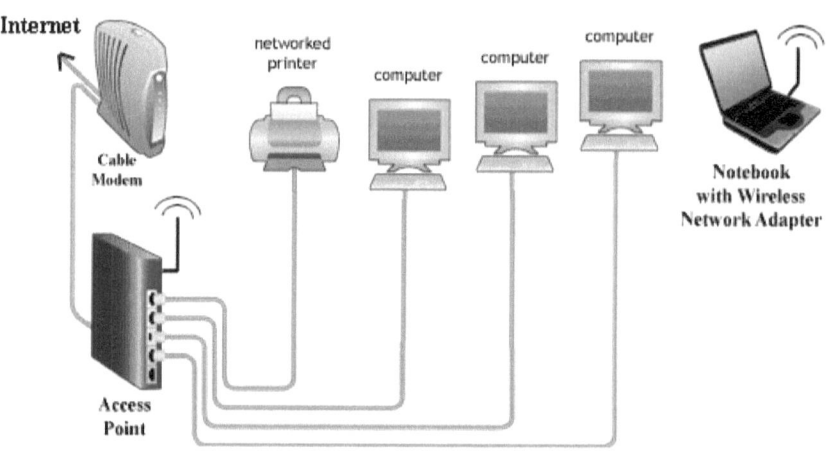

mple home network

A simple network at home consists roughly of a service provider's modem, and possibly a separate router and/or switch, and 1 or more computing devices to give you access. We don't use phone lines!(the DSL phone wire, is the only exception, hooks up to the DSL service modem and nothing else) Ethernet wires and their RJ-45 jacks (looking like telephone-but not) is the stuff that hooks up your local network.

Printers, VoIP phones, Home security cameras, computers, notebooks, TVs, tablets, cellphones, wireless access points (WAP), and now even some newer household appliances can be members of a computer network.

Here is some helpful jargon:

The IP address - A local IP looks like 192.168.1.123. Almost every device in a computer network has a IP address, but there's more to it than that. First, a ISP gives customers a specific IP address which identifies them online. This is a wide area network (WAN) IP. If you expect to use more than 1 device online this IP needs to become a corridor to a mini IP network on the customer's end. This is called a local area network (LAN).

Subnetting - Ok, now that one IP that gets assigned and becomes a corridor or 'gateway' to a separate LAN network, is what's called being subnetted. Think of subnetting as breaking up 1 IP into a bunch of different IPs. This is all done seamlessly within a LAN network using network address translation(NAT) and the address resolution protocol(ARP).

Dynamic Host Configuration Protocol (DHCP) - store bought routers will automatically assign IP's to computer devices whether wired or wireless. This is its internal DHCP server at work.

WAN - Wide Area Network. This is the ISP's own network and is the one that gets you online internet service and knows you by, among other things, the IP address assigned to you in this network.

LAN - Local Area Network. This is everything the customer has plugged in after the service modem and is inside of the customer's personal network. Its customary to have LAN IP's as 192.168.[network#].[host] where network# is usually 1 (but can be anything between 0-255) just as long as its consistently used on all LAN devices. [host#] is unique to each LAN device and can either get set automatic by DHCP or manually. Host # can be anything from 1-254.

Setting Up Network Hardware - Most any computer network peripherals can be configured through a built-in management page and sometimes by command line. Hookup to the equipment by HTTP or TELNET, connect network wires. You might have to manually configure IP, subnet, and gateway and use IP scanner or wireshark to ping or sniff out network to find out LAN IPs. (Many store bought routers are at default IP of 192.168.1.1/24). Open a web browser and type something like 'http://192.168.1.1' in the address bar. The factory defaults of most of these devices have a predictable username and password. Some hardware like manageable switches and routers, have a *console* port for serial cable hookup. Connect a PC up to this and use terminal software(hypertrm.exe).

Service Modem - This is the first essential thing. Unlike 300 or 2400 baud modems of yesteryear, these are usually the property of a service provider and can't be tampered with. To use a analogy, Think of it as a pay TV box. The box can be plugged into your computer or (another) router device through the RJ-45 jacks which are the all too common ethernet wires we discussed earlier. Newer service modems now have router and wireless functionality built in and likewise give you 4 or 8 jacks/ports to plug devices into.

Home router - The very common, and even old 10Mbit/100Mbit/Gigabit 4-port home routers, by Linksys, Belkin, D-link, and others. If you don't have one laying around, find these used or in dumpsters. Either with or without wireless, they usually have 5 ports in the back. One port plugs into the WAN network or ISP modem and the 4 other ports plug into 4 different network devices. Most store bought network hardware, like routers, have a internal web based user interface reachable through your web browser. Once things are plugged in and set to the same subnet you should be able to reach this. Its important that one become acquainted with this. It can even save you the hassle of having to go through a unnecessary run-around that helps the less tech savvy use the product. Regular store bought network-ready things like routers will tell you in the manual that you have to install their software on each computer but a lot of times, you don't need to do this.

From a web browser you can type the unit's default assigned LAN IP in the address bar to open up a management page provided everything's connected by ethernet and powered up. example: http://192.168.1.1

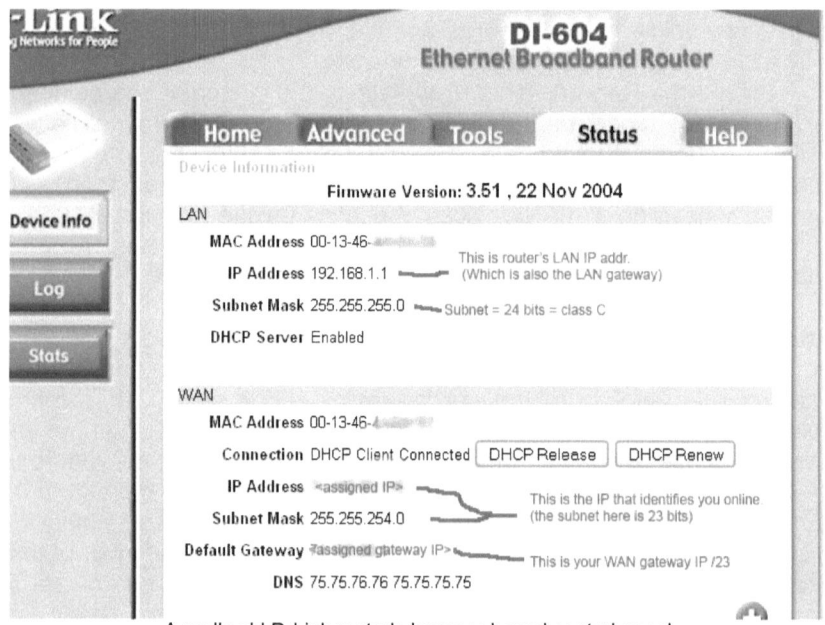

A really old D-Link router's browser based control panel

Wireless Routers(wifi) - These are common nowadays. Most 2.4Ghz wireless radio transceiver routers support modes A,B,G, and even N. Each device that connects to your access point by radio becomes a full-fledged member of your LAN just as much as wired clients. If you expect to not have

56

your LAN compromised by hackers - Leaving open wifi is up to you. If you don't want any intruders on your network, turn on WPA or WPA2 scrambling with AES. Set your own passphrase. Not broadcasting the SSID name, is a good idea but that alone will not fool everyone. Many routers have a special guest mode for wireless hosts that limits access.

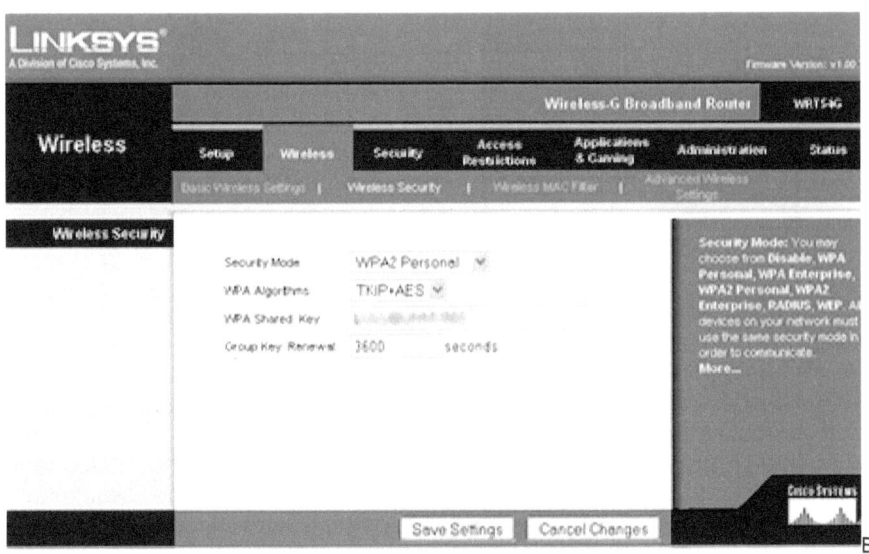

xample of a router's wireless security settings

Resetting and/or logging into network equipment - Like routers, other network-ready things almost always have a settings/management page reachable by opening its IP on a web browser. Default IPs are usually something like 192.168.1.X and X could be any host between 1-254. It may ask for a username and password. On used equipment you should reset/wipe the memory as you might not know what the past owner settings and passwords were. Look for a small hole or button on the side or bottom that might say reset. Follow the 60 - 60 rule and hold the reset button down 60 seconds with the power connected, and hold the button for 60 more secs. with the power unplugged. This should wipe the device to factory condition. Now connect this to network and from a web browser type in a 192.168.[0,1,or 2].1. Use *Angry IP scanner* to locate router's IP. These things almost always have a really obvious default username and password like "admin" and "password" or sometimes just "admin" and a blank password. The user manual might give it away too. Also, hackers occasionally publish lists of default logins by devices brand/model. Below is just a few to give you the drift:

User	Password
admin	password
Admin	Password
admin	admin
admin	1234
admin	

Some probable default logins. Experiment here.

Switches - If someone needs to plug more network devices into ethernet, you have to use a switch. Hubs are the obsolete cousin to a switch. A store bought consumer grade switch has 4, 8, or more jacks/ports. One ethernet data cable plugs between a LAN side port on a router or service modem and a port marked outbound WAN(sometimes port 1) on the switch/hub. Computers and network devices then plug into the remaining LAN ports.

Firewall - This is a piece of hardware equipment that has a management page. Filters traffic between your network and the cloud. Hooks up as the first device. Has inbound and outbound ports . Also like a home router they have a management web page built in. Here you should be able to block ports, packet types, etc. Many store bought routers have basic port blocking built in already so... They are really best suited if you have a larger than normal private network with vulnerable computers and a lot at stake.

You need an IP address - Under normal conditions, your PC or anything else will get assigned a IP by your local network's DHCP server. This should happen seamlessly in a matter of a minute or less. If not, open network connections and then right click and go to 'status'. That shows your IP info (if any). If you have no IP address you are not communicating. In order to connect with your router's network (and to reach its mgmt. page) you may need to manually enter IP settings into Windows until you fix the settings.

By the way, when doing any offline work, should you ever see 127.0.0.1 or the domain 'localhost', thats called a loopback and it means your within your own *local* machine. You would find this out when serving your own websites, email, ftp, database, and so on.

Helpful commands for configuring and testing network.

ipconfig Displays current IP settings.

`ipconfig /release` - Releases auto IP settings

`ipconfig /renew` - Automatically renews IP settings

`ipconfig /flushdns` - Wipes DNS cache.

ping <IP addr.> - the classic way of telling if another computer/device is reachable on a network. Displays packets returned and delay in ms.

`ping 192.168.1.1` - lists results

tracert<IP addr> - kind of like ping on steroids. this not only tells if a endpoint is reachable but also tells you about all the other devices or 'hops' it had to go through to reach that destination IP.

`tracert 192.168.1.1` - lists results

netstat - Lists the communication status of running tasks. Many switches. shows port#, status, <src IP>, <dst IP>, process ID, TCP/UDP, ...lists open ports, and other. Good for getting a glimpse of your running tasks to see what they're up to.

arp - displays and modifies the IP-to-physical address translation tables used by address resolution protocol(ARP).
syntax: arp -a [inet_addr] [-N if_addr]
  `arp -a`
displays current ARP entries.
  `arp -s 157.55.85.212 00-aa-00-62-c6-09`
  Adds a static entry.

netsh – Lots of options. *netsh* is a bit too advanced but gets you into net shell where you can configure IP settings by command prompt.

Setting IP Manually - You have to do this in your admin account. Go into Network connections > [choose one] > properties > TCP/IP properties page. on the TCP/IP settings tab, (you would probably see the IP address and the DNS IP address set to Automatic) switch both to manual and make the needed changes. The IP needs to be on the same network as the router's LAN IP. A good example is shown below:

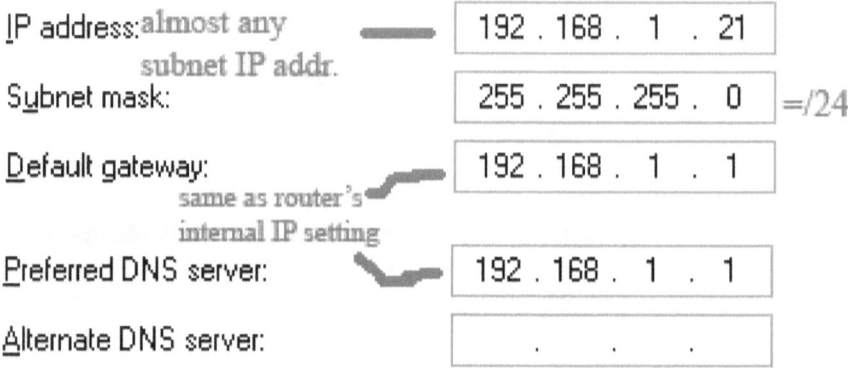

manual settings would look something like this

Now click Apply and Ok out of everything. The setting get applied when you ok and close out of network connections properties. If it all just starts working soon afterwards, log out of Admin and log into User before testing the web surfing capabilities.

Using Window's Built-in Wireless Support - Most every laptop has a wireless network card. With the computer's wireless drivers already installed and working, Windows has built-in support for WiFi. Right-click the wireless computer icon in the tray area and select View Available Wireless Networks. Next, you might see your own wireless router detected. To add a access point(AP) name + its wireless settings to the list click the 'Change The Order Of Preferred Networks' left side link. (or else wait for the AP to be detected by periodically clicking the 'Check Available Networks' top-left side link). In the Preferred networks section of the 'Wireless Network Connection Properties' page is a list of access points that windows already detected or were manually filled in. It best to do this manually if router doesn't broadcast its name or have a specific encryption type + password. So either click Add... or choose your router name from the list and click properties to edit.

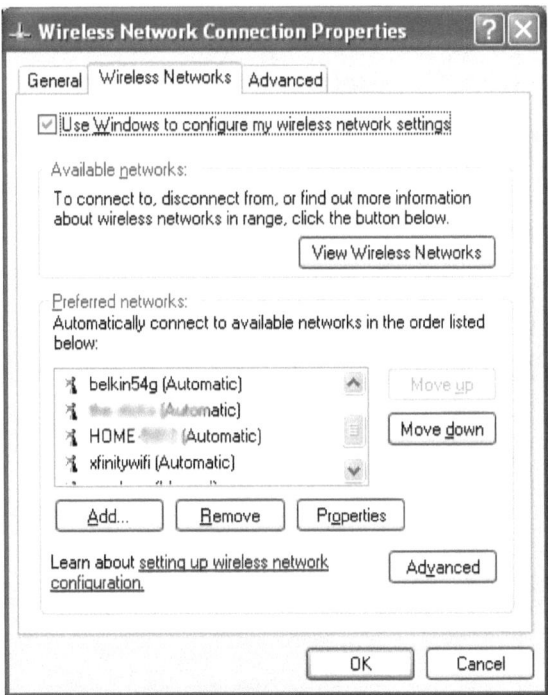

Wireless Network Connection Properties

The next properties sheet will let you fill in specifics of a wireless - Even if not broadcasting.

<SSID name> Properties

Click Ok when done then go to the Wireless Network Connections page while clicking refresh occasionally. The wireless network should be detected and connected in a minute. If everything works you'll see the little computer icon in the system tray WITHOUT a 'x' on it and showing signs of activity. it should light up soon afterwards. Right-click that icon and select Status... The status popup should indicate its connected, bytes sent/received, and IP settings.

Using a 3rd-party wireless client software - Sometimes a manufacturer will supply there own wireless utility software. It handles the detection and security details instead of Windows Wireless Zero(which must be disabled to avoid conflict). Some wireless utilities are good, a some aren't and end up being a hassle.

IP version 6 - Its been getting phased in for years. IPv6 has been planned decades ago. Addresses are 128bits long, that's 4 times bigger than conventional IPs. IPv6 addresses display as 8 groups of 32-bit hexadecimal values as apposed to IPv4's 4, 8-bit decimal numbers.

a entire, unabbreviated IPv6 address takes the form of:

```
1234:5678:9ABC:DEF0:1234:5678:9ABC:DEF0
```

A loopback/localhost IPv6 IP looks like:

`0:0:0:0:0:0:0:1` or just `::1`.

Windows XP has a built-in service/protocol for IPv6 (IPv6 NetBIOS, WINS?) but **not sure what that does for you**. I noticed IPv6 in effect either way but for what its worth, to install this component, go into Network connections and the Connection Properties for one of the connection items. Click Install and then choose 'Protocol' and Choose TCP/IP version 6.

You may notice that your new v6 IP takes and uses the numbers from your network card's MAC sddress, and this is normal. Periodically changing your version 6 IP could prove useful down the road...

Bluetooth - Is a shorter-range form of wireless designed for computing accessories like earphones, microphones, iPods, whatever else. Currently real popular as Apple products and smart phone accessories. Bluetooth was always around and most wireless-G NIC's support Bluetooth. wired vs. wireless, you decide but to reduce unnecessary overhead and it does present a security risk from crafty hackers as these things can allegedly be broken into easier than wifi, go into services, and disable the obvious Bluetooth service then go into msconfig.exe and disable any background utilities pertaining to Bluetooth. Reboot for change to take effect.

GPS tracking - If you're not into being geolocated, its usually optional if supported at all. This could be toggled in the driver's property page. As admin run devmgmt.msc, locate your NIC in the device list, click this and maybe under the *Advanced* tab, find a setting for GPS and change that. Adjust or disable any background programs for GPS if there is any and reboot.

Network Troubleshooting:
There may be a time when you need to spy out your own network to find bottlenecks and their causes. below is a few ways to do that.

Using Netstat – For starters, the easiest command ever, `netstat -a -b` tells you running tasks and their networking characteristics.

Using a IP Scanner - Angry IP Scanner helps feel out a LAN network. Its a free product. You can do a class C IP scan to find out which IPs are being used by a computer or other device. Note - if you have a souped up XP with the TCP/IP patch installed, With some adjustments Angry IP scanner can do its scans much faster.

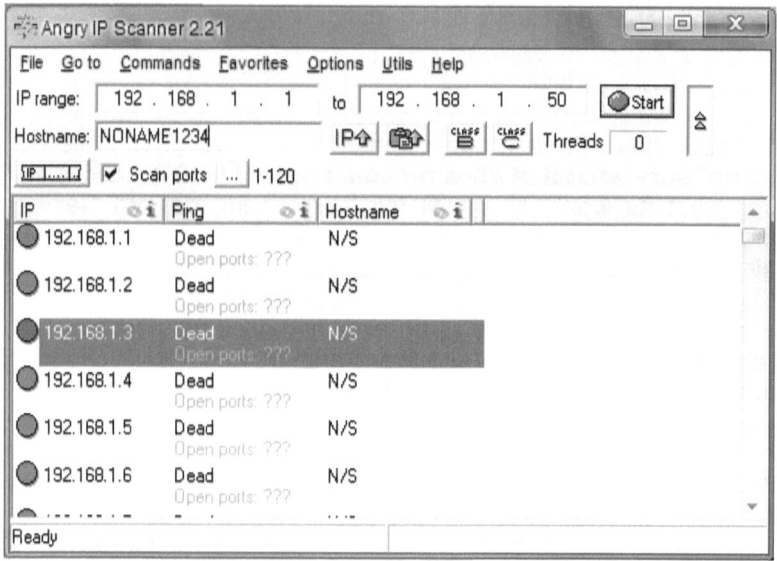

Network Analysis - Wireshark is a popular *packet sniffing* program for viewing and logging network activity. It will capture and list the protocols and break down the meaning of every single byte in that transmission, by network layer. A listing of network protocols is in appendix C.

Chapter 6 - Being E-Street Wise

Careful! Don't install/execute all the new software - Look out for software that tries to assert its for your own good. Any software you have running with admin privileges has the power to take over everything in your computer!

The following things should be avoided:

- **TROJAN HORSE -** Many times cyber-hooligans send a official or legit looking email or setup websites (with a vague look of phony) that trick unsuspecting computer users into downloading and running a .exe file, sometimes even automatically. if the hacker's script gets write access to critical files, that script can then plant a machine language program somewhere (and disguise it as a normal windows system file). The machine language executable may not even do anything at first but by then its too late and you'll need to do system restore, run virus scanner, or even a clean re-install to fix this.
- **A freely offered software with strings attached -** They look good at first but after the software is installed, comes with auto updaters, quick starters, or other scheduled "maintenance" programs, registration form popups, too much network activity, or just slows down computer. If you must use one of these, be careful during installation and opt out of any unwanted features like free anti-virus or whatever else they have in mind.
- **Defective -** This is just something that honestly doesn't work right. Shows signs of being "Bloatware" or buggy, memory leaking, has too many pop-ups, and locks up or hogs up system. Don't want.

Prevent yourself from opening questionable executables or anything like that, batch scripts, or anything else you are unsure of. Remember a couple chapters ago i told you to enable showing of file extensions, hidden, and system files in the 'Folder Options' in your admin account? Do the same thing in your regular account too! Just remember that when you go to rename a file icon you have to provide the extension as well(or your icon will change!). Be sure your mouse clicker works well - and doesn't cause double clicks that you didn't mean to do. Image and text files are usually real safe. Sometimes there are other exploitabilities when opening files in popular software. MS office used to run VB scripts automatically, thereby allowing malicious scripts to have their way. PDF readers and other big software of this caliber also have script processing features. These should be disabled if you can. Even the old 'Windows Media Player' allowed embedded scripts to run and wreak havoc so use a different media player. Be on guard for anything with extensions like .reg, .js, .vb, .bat, .com, .bin, and last but not least .exe.

Web Browsing Safely From Admin Account

If you must be a full-admin user, after all you can't change network settings as user, this is how to do it. Remember how i said the web browser is the most vulnerable thing? Well it is. Microsoft Certification courses even teach this. Use 'runas' command to run your web browser of choice, and all its plugins, under Windows restrictions, that is at minimum, not being able to write, modify, or delete critical system files - which is what most hijacker websites count on.

You'll need a fully configured browser in one of your limited user accounts.

First, open up shortcut properties. Copy the target filename(Paste in Notepad if needed), The 1st runas param. should be a non-admin acct. and the 2nd, the original target that you just copied. Create a new limited user or guest acct(if you dont already have it) and set up your browser of choice in that account.

```
runas <guest/limited user acct.> "<shortcut target>"
```
for example, it would look like:
```
runas /user:COMPUTERNAM\User "C:\Program Files\Mozilla
Firefox\firefox.exe"
```

After you are done, This shortcut should now function, with or without asking for a password. The icon will change to the system default so to fix that, you can click 'Change Icon..' in properties page and browse your c:\program files directory for the browsers appropriate icon, this can even be the executable itself.

Now you have a shortcut to your User accounts version of Firefox.

Note that when up/downloading files, they will all get saved in the file space of that limited user only and won't be able to access your administrator desktop or my documents. You would have to later copy them, so as they inherit the permissions of the parent folder. Never move files from one user account to another, but copy it instead.

Avoid crappy search bars and other gadgets – I know nobody likes getting plug-ins planted in their browser just from visiting a website. They often promote these as a new toolbar like a search feature or a live feed gadget. Keeping watch of what plug-ins belong and which ones need to be removed is very important. These settings, listing all the plug-ins or extensions installed, should be reachable and manageable by you. Plug-ins for Microsoft Media Player should be turned off. In Firefox, its easy enough to do this and uninstall any add-ons you don't need. Microsoft DRM plugins can be turned off too but sometimes websites require you to use their special plugin to download their wares.

Hey, Free apps! - Do you have any favorite browser extensions or add-ons? Keep them offline when possible. Firefox. XPI files and Chrome .CRX files are capable of being saved.

Cookies - Cookies are necessary pieces of data a website stores in your browser. They allow the storage of login info with scrambled identifiers of your login status so you stay logged on. Some cookies are completely unwanted, like what you get from advertisements and tracking cookies. Erasing cookies occasionally is a good way to keep these annoying things out of your browser. Cookies are usually time sensitive, but not always. Remember to keep logins to websites **written down** so you don't need to rely on cookies or saved passwords in your browser. Adobe Flash and possibly other plug-ins can also store information in your browser too and its good to wipe your browser cache occasionally as well as any 3rd party plug-in data. Set your browser to wipe out everything when needed, do it frequently. Wiping out your cookies is the best way to opt out of advertiser tracking you.

Online Anonymity?

Every file created with your computer, whether video, PDF, even images and document files can have traceable metadata plastered in the header. Windows PC's are designed by nature to leave a ePaper trail.

Even if you got windows locked down, 3rd party software and adware installed in your machine can put out beacons online thereby blowing your cover. Be aware of all your own background software and use wireshark to see what the heck you're putting out there before moving on in this endeavor.

Every computer with a IP can be traced. Not only that but your giving away many more tidbits in a online session than you think - all of which combine to make up your browser signature. Some unique information is given up by you during each web page request like:

REMOTE_IP/HOST/PORT - your IP, host name, or port #,
HTTP_USER_AGENT - the kind of browser and OS you're using,
HTTP_REFERER - the last webpage you visited.

HTTP Headers look roughly like this:

```
HTTP_HOST:<any website>
HTTP_USER_AGENT:Mozilla/5.0 (Windows; …..
HTTP_ACCEPT:text/html,application/xhtml+xml,application/
xml
HTTP_ACCEPT_LANGUAGE:en-us,en;
HTTP_ACCEPT_ENCODING:gzip,deflate
HTTP_ACCEPT_CHARSET:ISO-xxxx,utf-8;q=xx,*;q=xx
HTTP_KEEP_ALIVE:xxx
HTTP_CONNECTION:keep-alive
PATH: < xxxxx >
COMSPEC:C:\WINDOWS\system32\cmd.exe
PATHEXT:.COM;.EXE;.BAT;.CMD;.VBS;.VBE;.JS;.JSE;.WSF;.WSH
WINDIR:C:\WINDOWS
SERVER_SIGNATURE:
SERVER_SOFTWARE:Apache/x.x.xx (Win32) PHP/x.x.x.x
SERVER_NAME:localhost
SERVER_ADDR:127.0.0.1
SERVER_PORT:80
REMOTE_ADDR:127.0.0.1
DOCUMENT_ROOT:C:/xxxxx
SERVER_ADMIN:xyz@somewebsite.com
SCRIPT_FILENAME:C:/xxxxxxx/index.php
REMOTE_PORT:xxxxx
GATEWAY_INTERFACE:CGI/1.1
SERVER_PROTOCOL:HTTP/1.1
REQUEST_METHOD:GET
QUERY_STRING:
REQUEST_URI:/
SCRIPT_NAME:/index.php
PHP_SELF:/index.php
REQUEST_TIME:xxxxxxxxxxx
```

Anonymizer websites, proxy servers, and *Tor Browser* can guard your privacy. You'll see the web in a different way. These would be neat years ago and would fool the websites at that time. Sometimes this comes in handy but the web in general is a dynamic thing and tends to adapt to this form of hiding. Due to abuse, some websites even blacklist the known Tor IPs. Also, the proxyfied page request many times are rendered so crudely its almost not worth it.

To use a proxy server, look them up first since they tend to change a lot. Anonimizer sites offer lists of free proxy servers to try. Input the proxy server into your browser's settings and switch to proxy mode. Supply the proxy IP and port number and your set. In any case, its a higher level of being secret but the HTTP metadata your browser gives away, your IP address, and everything else kind of blows it ultimately.

Why computers are so vulnerable and whats a firewall?

PC's and Apple products were meant to be very user friendly - and allowing full control for advertisement marketing gimmicks. These obscurities allow in everything flashy, sometimes to the point of giving you the business. That is why *default permit* is wrecking so many people's reputations and hard drive contents all the time.

Suppose you were someone who didn't need any specialized software for network book keeping, gaming, teleconferencing or what have you - nothing except use web browser software. A firewall can filter out a whole lot of garbage going in and out of your machine. The *cloud* and its HTML5 based interfaces are the thing now right? You would still be able to watch streaming video, check news and weather, download files, and so on. Only a small number of ports are needed to facilitate this.

For our purposes, a data transmission consists of:

[your IP #] [your port #] < ------send data to / from ------- > [server IP #] [server port #]

Initially we want to filter all data going in and out - as in block all communication, incoming/outgoing, except for a few critical port numbers. A firewall would permit based on the port # on the server's end, not yours. Unless you're serving web pages, your port number, at your end is a arbitrary number. The bare minimal server requests you need for web browsing consists of:

Block all IP traffic except for the following:		
Server port	**Application protocol**	**Protocol**
80	Hypertext – HTTP	TCP
443	Secure Hypertext – HTTPS (TCP, SSL, OCSP, TLSv1)	TCP
53	Resolving domain names - DNS	UDP
67,68	Automatic IP config(from your own LAN) – DHCP	UDP

Program this into your local firewall device if its possible, and permit more ports as you need them for email, telnet, ftp, online games, phone and video communication, or whatever else. For example, do you automatically need your time set? port 123 needs to be opened for that.

Software Firewalls? - Windows Firewall is inadequate and only prevents inbound traffic but you don't need any special firewall software. The ability to block or allow ports is a hidden ability of NT but not taught to the general public.

TCP/IP Filtering? - You may have seen this under TCP/IP's advanced settings. Go to *Internet Connections* and open the properties. Double-click or open properties for the ***Internet protocol(TCP/IP)*** network item and on the resulting properties pop-up click on the ***advanced...*** button. Go to the *Options* tab on *Advanced TCP/IP settings* properties and open up ***TCP/IP Filtering*** in Optional settings. but if it works at all, its really not what we want to use. Its never worked right so I disfavor its use completely.

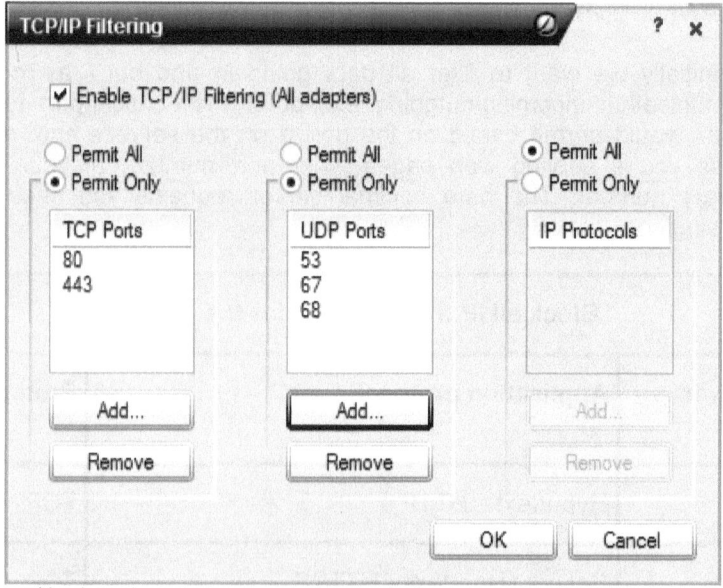

You have to restart your computer each time you make changes!

Firewalling With IPSEC - This technique worked in the Windows 2000 days and is much easier to manage afterwards. Infact, works all kinds of better than the TCP/IP Filtering.

  - First, run secpol.msc OR run mmc.exe and add snap-in for *IP Security Policies*.

You first have to add filters and actions. Right click on the IP security policies node in the left hand navigation pane and in the context menu, choose *Manage IP filter lists and filter actions.* A window pops up. On the *filter actions* tab, you'll see built-in actions like require or request security, and permit. Click **Add,** a new action popup is shown. Lets call this action **BLOCK**. On the *Security Methods* tab, select the **Block** option and hit apply and ok out.

Note: Whenever you see a checkbox for *Use Add Wizard* uncheck that.

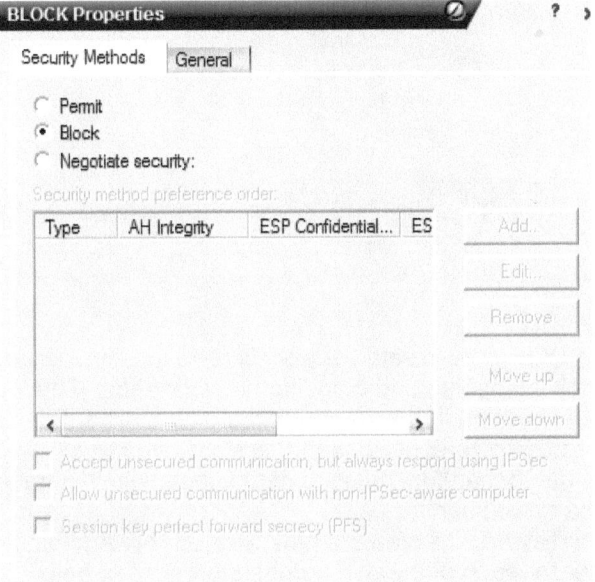

Creating Filters - You should next have a BLOCK action listed along with the others. Now switch into the *manage IP Filter Lists* tab. Add a new filter list by clicking *Add.* A filter list actually contains many filters, so you have to create the single filters one at a time. Click Add again to create your single filter. Since you want to first block all traffic, all ports and IPs, from your computer to any computer(and visa-versa so leave mirror checked), the defaults should work. click (apply and) ok, then lastly name you filter list something like BLOCK ALL, verify everything looks right(like in the image shown below) and OK out.

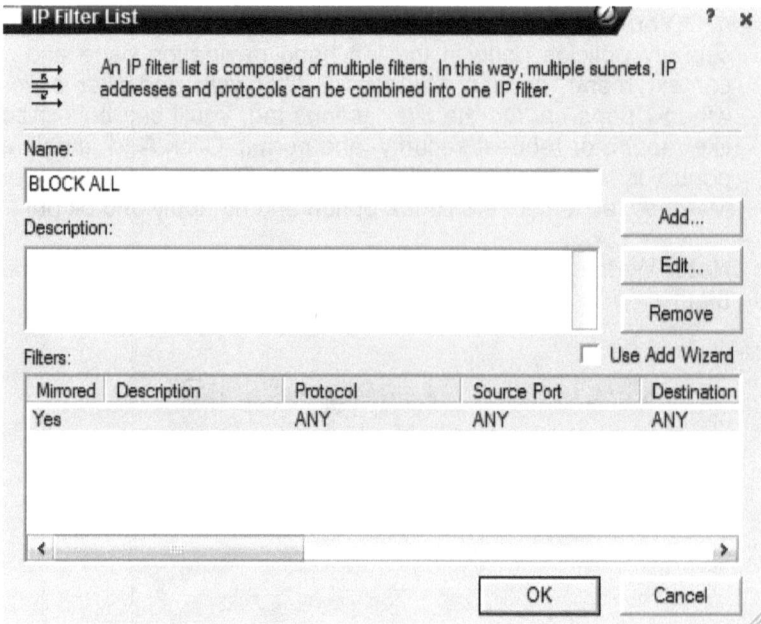

You now created a filter that takes the action of BLOCK, to block all ingoing and outgoing network traffic. The BLOCK ALL filter list should be in there with all the others. The next filter list is going to to be more specific, and therefore overlap the BLOCK rule(when we get to that!). Its going to permit the minimal number of ports to be able to web surf.

Hit 'Add' to create a new filter list, hit 'Add' again, and create a filter for each of the port numbers prescribed below. On the first tab, you see something like *your IP* to *Any IP,* and the *Mirrored* checkbox. Leave these as is. The next tab, the source port # is arbitrary and can be left *Any*. The destination port #, the *endpoint* is what we want to single out. You need to create 5 filter items for TCP ports 80, 443, and UDP ports 53, 67, and 68. One filter for each port #. After all that, you should see a list of all the filters you created, verify that these are all correct.

An IP filter list is composed of multiple filters. In this way, multiple subnets, IP addresses and protocols can be combined into one IP filter.

Name:

PERMIT BARE MINIMAL

Description:

Add...

Edit...

Remove

Filters: ☐ Use Add Wi

Mirrored	Description	Protocol	Source Port	Destination Port
Yes		TCP	ANY	80
Yes		TCP	ANY	443
Yes		UDP	ANY	53
Yes		UDP	ANY	67
Yes		UDP	ANY	68

Finally, name your filter list something like PERMIT BARE MINIMAL and hit OK. OK out of Manage Lists and Actions and go on to the next step.

Creating the Policy - On the left pane, Right click to *Create a IP security policy* and go on to the IP Security Policy Wizard. Name your policy item something like FIREWALL, click Next, uncheck the *activate the default response rule*, hit Next and Finish to edit your *policy's rule* (or you can do that later, without wizard clicking *Add)*.

Creating Rules - The rule items you need to create here will first tell Windows NT to block all network communication and then allow in only a select few protocols needed to lease your IP, receive DNS (so http links work with names instead of raw IPs), and ports 80 and 443 allow in HTTP, HTTPS requests. Because of policy physics, the rules of a narrower scope overlaps the block all rule, which is much broader scope.

You want all network connections, no IPSEC tunnel, and the filter lists and the actions tabs set using the BLOCK action and the filter lists you already made up. The following 2 rule items need to be created (with Add):

Filter list	Action
BLOCK ALL	BLOCK
PERMIT BARE MINIMAL	Permit

Ok out and make sure only these new rules you created are checked. Finally, make sure your policy is named something and Apply and/or OK out.

Text representation of *policies*:

[1 filter item]
|
[Filter list(=many filters)]   [1 Action(permit, block, require security)]
\   /
[1 Rule item]
|
[1 Policy item(= Many Rules)]

Assign Your FIREWALL Policy - Captain Kirk knows when to call shields up before being in range of attack by Romulans or Klingons but to drop shields so non-hostile guests can come aboard. Likewise your new firewall can be toggled on and off. You must first right click on it and choose *Assign* for firewall to be active.

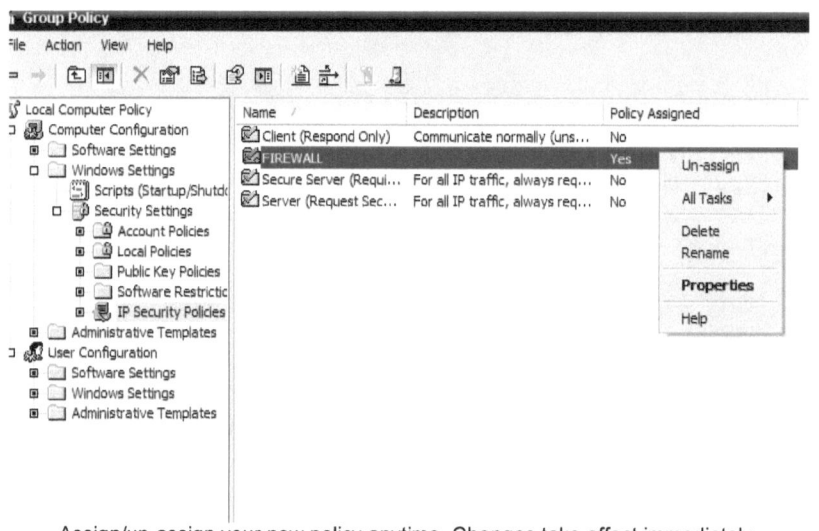

Assign/un-assign your new policy anytime. Changes take affect immediately.

Finally, if you are in MMC, before closing Management Console, Save your console template to your administrator desktop. Call it something like FIREWALL.msc and open this console to control or make changes whenever you need to. You don't need to reboot. Changes take effect immediate or in a small, matter of minutes, timeframe

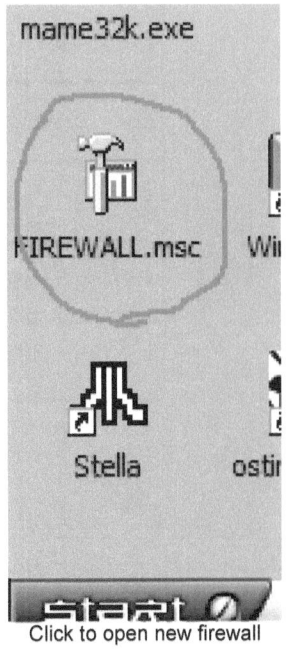

Click to open new firewall

Testing - Test to see that your assigned FIREWALL policy is really operating. First try to use your web browser to see if that works while FIREWALL policy is assigned. Next, try using something like POP3 email, ftp, telnet, sip, online chat or whatever uses something besides ports 80 or 443. You shouldn't be able to get though either way when firewall is assigned. Assign/un-assign FIREWALL, see how things work with or without the FIREWALL policy assigned. You should see a difference. Unlike windows firewall, this firewall policy blocks not just inbound but anything initiated by your own computer's software and you wont get any annoying alerts when a block occurs. Add more permit filters as you need them for your particular software. Lists of software port # assignments is in appendix C but you may need to packet sniff to see what port numbers are required to be open. Blocking by IP addresses can also come in handy. Suppose you have a software product that forces you to visit their website. You can block/blacklist their IP and not only hinder annoying nag screens but also not be getting tracked.

Advanced Bonus - There is still a chance of DNS spoofing from uncertified DNS servers. I have a simple solution. If your DNS is limited to LAN, it will have to default to your gateway's IP for DNS and this should work in most cases. Break down the PERMIT rule into 2 separate rules, with one configured for LAN only connections. Add a LAN only rule and change your filters accordingly.

Filter List	Action	Con. Type
BLOCK ALL	BLOCK	All
PERMIT DNS 53	Permit	LAN Only
PERMIT DHCP 67,68	Permit	LAN Only
PERMIT HTTP 80, 443	Permit	All

Correcting Normal Windows Bugs

Once in awhile you may get stuck in a Windows process or something that causes the operating system to be overloaded or infinitely looped. Its not necessarily a virus. Explorer's file search sometimes holds up, any long lengthy file copy/move/metadata change process that you inadvertently started not knowing it would take hours, or sometimes just the classic infinite loop. Experience is the best teacher and sometimes you can wait these out but who knows how long. This situation can usually be remedied without rebooting the computer.

Windows Explorer - Or explorer.exe is your file management system, as you know it. It populates the desktop icons and folder windows and lets you navigate anywhere in your file system. If something goes berserk, you can fix the problem by restarting *explorer.exe*. Note that 2 instances of explorer cannot be ran at the same time.

Do this:
- Run task manager, go to *Processes* tab.
- End process *explorer.exe*. the desktop will then disappear.
- Go to *Applications* tab and click *New Task...* enter in explorer.exe and ok to confirm. your desktop should be loading back in.

The *Your certificates are invalid* problem – Suppose one day you open up your Facebook account only to find out you cant. Instead you get a popup about invalid websites certificates. You click though and add the exception but yet it still wont work. You say to yourself, "what's wrong?" and you go search Google for help only to get no Google but instead the same kind message about expired/invalid certificate. in fact just about every website you visit starts blocking you this way, "what?" you say as you begin to totally freak out.

Solution - Windows time and date. You're not even on the right year! Go set the date month and year correctly, maybe even reboot, and everything should start working like normal again.

Hanging print jobs in printer queue – Occasionally a printer will stop responding because of Windows software problems, not just the printer itself. This is a easy fix; **reboot and the lost print jobs all start happening afterwards.** Then there's times you just can't reboot because you'll loose all your work. Similar to how we fixed issues with explorer lockups, Its possible to reset the print queue by going into Task Manager and under *Processes* stop *spoolsv.exe* (and even others possibly) then under *Application* start New Task *spoolsv.exe*. Hopefully printer will respond seconds later.

Becoming a certified hacker? – Cyber-criminals usually get to perform their dirty works over and over again. *Shadow computing* is the new tactical approach to security. There is training needed to do this kind of work, along with computer forensics. In *Certified Ethical Hacker Study Guide* they teach you the ropes, so that's something to get into once you first master not being hacked.

Chapter 7 - Choosing Another Operating System

So you might not like to use something being end-of-lifed out of existence and want to look for something better and different. Linux perhaps? There are some non-linux alternatives too. Here's the top options, (Special thanks to the respective online authors for the information)

Starting with Windows:

- Windows Embedded - Commercial - Is a compact version of Windows. Older versions must go on working as there is necessity to continue supporting this platform as many kiosk and ATMs and so on, can't just simply be upgraded. With the software itself and the how tos, Windows Embedded can be ran on a PC.

- Windows 7,8,10 PE or minimal version - FREE -They supposedly make these special, scale down builds of windows just for getting practice on. They might just run faster and have less overhead than the full commercial versions.

- Windows Server - Commercial - In server, you get to choose roles like DNS server, web server with IIS, and Active Directory and what is the stuff that lets you be master of your (MS) domain??? Server is designed for any number of instances of windows user sessions to run concurrently, even remote desktop. Think of Server as a beefed up windows as it gives you more concurrent connections, perform VPN networking, and be your own CA.The bad part of Server is not just trying to get compatible drivers but all the red tape you may run into down the road. If you want all the roles and functionality, use highest version. Good luck Contoso!

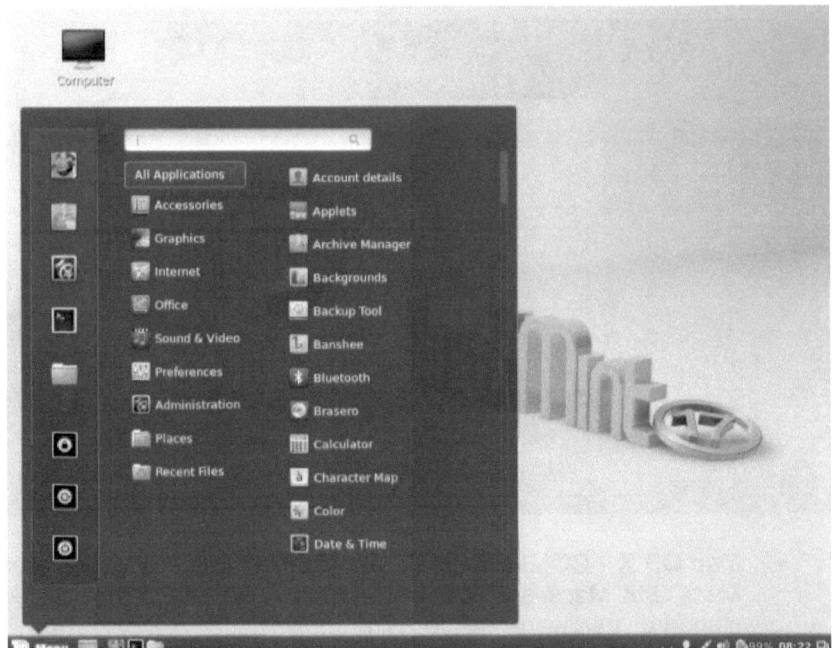

- Mint - FREE/OPEN SOURCE. - Might be one of the most preferred Linux distros out there now. Mint is a Linux distribution built on top of Ubuntu. It uses Ubuntu's software repositories, so the same packages are available on both. Originally, Mint was an alternative distribution loved mainly because it included media codecs and proprietary software that Ubuntu didn't include by default.This distribution now has its own identity and some Ubuntu developers label it insecure.

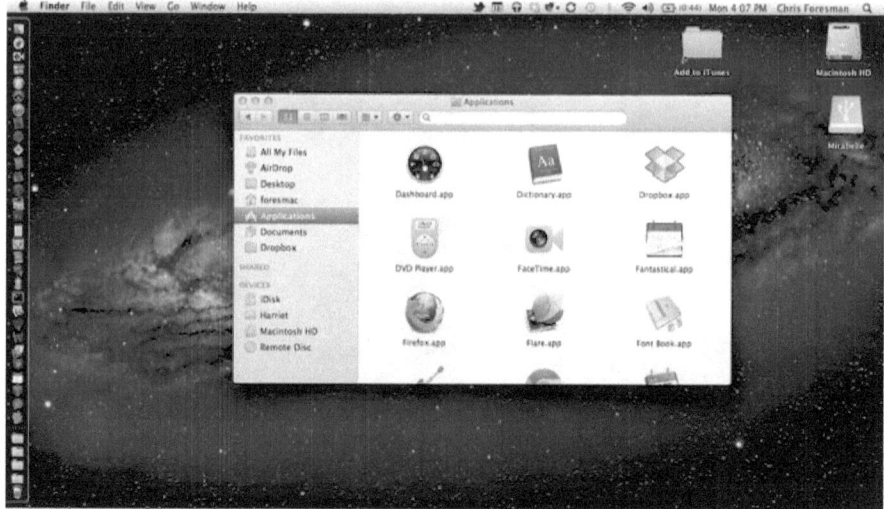

- Mac OS X - COMMERCIAL - Apple's Mac OS X is preinstalled on Macs, but Macs are now just another type of PC with the same standard hardware inside. The only thing stopping you from installing Mac OS X on a typical PC is Apple's license agreement and the way they limit their software. Mac OS X can run just fine on typical PCs if you can get around these restrictions. There's a thriving community of people building PCs that run Mac OS X — known as hackintoshes — out there.

- Chrome OS - COMMERCIAL/FREE (PAY AS YOU GO) – Yet another *Fisher Price* operating system is becoming more popular now than ever, Google's operating system "Built on the Linux kernel". Not really a full fledged operating system but is said to turn your PC into a 'ChromeBook' basically and can run chrome browser, apps, and everything else Google provides.

- Ubuntu - FREE/OPEN SOURCE - Ubuntu is probably the most well-known Linux distribution. Ubuntu is based on Debian, but it has its own software repositories. Much of the software in these repositories is synced from Debian's repositories. The Ubuntu project has a focus on providing a solid desktop (and server) experience, and it isn't afraid to build its own custom technology to do it. Ubuntu used to use the GNOME 2 desktop environment, but it now uses its own Unity desktop environment. Ubuntu is even building its own Mir graphical server while other distributions are working on the Wayland. Ubuntu is modern without being too bleeding edge. It offers releases every six months, with a more stable LTS (long term support) release every two years. Ubuntu is currently working on expanding the Ubuntu distribution to run on smart phones and tablets.

- Android - COMMERCIAL/FREE - Available for PC. This is the platform that popular Android phones and tablets run. Can't tell you any more than that.

- Solaris OS - COMMERCIAL(was free) - Solaris is a Unix operating system originally developed by Sun Microsystems. It superseded their earlier SunOS in 1993. Oracle Solaris, as it is now known, has been owned by Oracle Corporation since Oracle's acquisition of Sun in January 2010. (That means Solaris is no longer, exactly, open source or free)

- Fedora/Red Hat Linux - FREE(and commercial) - Fedora is a project with a strong focus on free software — you won't find an easy way to install proprietary graphics drivers here, although third-party repositories are available. Fedora is bleeding edge and contains the latest versions of software. Unlike Ubuntu, Fedora doesn't make its own desktop environment or other software. Instead, the Fedora project uses "upstream" software, providing a platform that integrates all this upstream software without adding their own custom tools or patching it too much. Fedora comes with the GNOME 3 desktop environment by default, although you can also get "spins" that come with other desktop environments. Fedora is sponsored by Red Hat, and is the foundation for the commercial Red Hat Enterprise Linux project. Unlike RHEL, Fedora is bleeding edge and not supported for long. If you want a more stable release that's supported for longer, Red Hat would prefer you use their Enterprise product(See CentOS for more info).

- SkyOS - COMMERCIAL(discontinued)/FREE - Unlike many of the other hobbyist operating systems here, SkyOS is proprietary and not open-source. You originally had to pay for access so you could use development versions of SkyOS on your own PC. Development on SkyOS ended in 2009, but the last beta version was made available as a free download in 2013.
- ReactOS - FREE/OPEN SOURCE - ReactOS is a free, open-source reimplementation of the Windows NT architecture. In other words, it's an attempt to reimplement Windows as an open-source operating system that's compatible with all Windows applications. A work in progress and has a long way to go catching up to Windows from the sound of it.

- eComStation - COMERCIAL - OS/2 was an operating system originally created by Microsoft and IBM. (there are still old ATMs, PCs, and other systems using OS/2) IBM no longer develops OS/2, but a company named Serenity Systems has the rights to continue distributing it.
- Debian - OPEN - Debian is an operating system composed only of free, open-source software. The Debian project has been operating since 1993 — over 20 years ago! This widely respected project is still releasing new versions of Debian, but it's known for moving much more slowly than distributions like Ubuntu or Linux Mint. This can make it more stable and conservative, which is ideal for some systems.

- Tons of other linux distros out there - openSUSE, Mageia / Mandriva, Arch, Slackware, and puppy linux just to name a few.

- Many more low-budget ongoing / discontinued operating system projects - Like Haiku - a reimplementation of BeOS, Syllable - an AmigaOS clone, FreeDOS, and SteamOS - a promising gaming OS and is actually a linux distro.

Appendix A - Windows Shortcut Keys

Probable BIOS and MS boot keys - These are keys used before the Windows graphic appears.	
F1, F2, DEL, ESC, CTRL+ALT+ESC, or CTRL+ALT+DEL	Enter BIOS Setup menu
F8 or F10	BIOS boot menu
F4	Starts MSDOS (obsolete)
F5 (or holding down shift)	Safe mode
F8	Options screen

Windows GUI Keys	
Mouse or other pointing device	
Movement	Moves pointer
Left click	Selects a file/object.
Left double click	Opens or runs a file/object.
Right click	Shows context/shortcut menu for selected item(s)
Mouse wheel control	Scrolls current document window.
Drag and drop	

<mouse drag>	Moves file/object(and its UAC settings)
CTRL+<mouse drag>	Copies file/object(inherits permissions of dest. parent folder)
ALT+<mouse drag>	Copies shortcut of file/object
NOTE:Some applications work as drop targets	
F2(or left click selection object)	Rename selected file/object
DEL key	Moves file/object to recycle bin
SHIFT+DEL	Delete selected file/object (No recycle bin)
WIN Key(or CNRL+ESC)	Opens start menu
APP key(or SHIFT+F10)	Opens context/shortcut menu. Almost same as right click.
Enter key	Selects,opens,or runs something.
Arrow keys(ARROWS)	Moves between items. Only 1 item is highlighted.
SHIFT + ARROWS	Moves between items and highlights a range of items.
ALT key	Toggles to application menu bar(or similar)

TAB or SHIFT+TAB	Skips to next or previous item.
ESC key	Escapes out of something (such as drop down menus)
F1 (or WIN+F1)	Displays help
F3	Starts find
F4	Open the drive selection when browsing
F5	Refresh contents(usually web browser)
F10	Reportedly can work the same as ALT(when not overrode)
ALT+<key>	Accelerator. Selects menu item with underlined letter.
ALT+TAB or ALT+SHIFT+TAB	Switches between running applications.
ALT+ESC	Switches to next running application.
WIN+TAB	Activate taskbar and cycle through buttons.
CNTL+TAB or CNTL+SHIFT+TAB OR CNTL+F6	Switches between child window/document (MDI apps).
ALT+F4	Close application with current focus.
CNTL+F4	Close child window/document within a application.

ALT+Spacebar	Displays control menu of current appliction.
ALT+Hyphen	Displays control menu of currently active child window/document within a application.
ALT+Enter	Display properties page of selected item(Or toggles between regular/full screen in a console app.)
CNTL+Z	Undo effect of last command.
ALT+Down Arrow	Displays contents of a drop-down list.
Print Screen Key	Copies entire screenshot to clipboard.
Print Screen Key + ALT	Copies screenshot of active window to clipboard.
WIN+M(or WIN+D)	Minimize all windows
Shift+WIN+M	Undo minimizing all windows
holding shift	Disables autoplay while first mounting a CD/DVD or flash drive.
WIN+Break	Opens System Properties page.
CNTL+SHIFT+ESC	Opens Task Manager.
WIN+F	File search
WIN+CTRL+F	Search for computers

WIN+R	Opens Run window
WIN+U	Utility Manager. Opens voice narrator, magnifier, or on-screen keyboard.
WIN+L	Locks (logout) computer
WIN+E	Open 'My Computer'

Universal Editing Keys

ARROWS or Mouse	Moves or re-positions cursor
Return key	Carriage return just like a typewriter.
Delete key(sometimes CTRL+X)	Deletes 1 character at cursor position(and shifts text back)
Insert key	Toggles between replace or insert mode editing.
ARROWS + SHIFT	Selects range of text while moving.
CTRL+LEFT ARROW or RIGHT ARROW(+ SHIFT)	Skips cursor at word increments. +shift causes text selection

PageUp or PageDown(+SHIFT)	Scrolls editing window in pages.
Home or End keys(+SHIFT)	Moves cursor to the beginning or end of a line.
CTRL+Home or CTRL+End(+SHIFT)	Move to beginning or end of entire document.
CTRL+A	Select all
CTRL+C or CTRL+Insert	Copy(anything) to clipboard.
CTRL+X or SHIFT+DEL	Cut (delete and copy to clipboard).
CTRL+V or SHIFT+Insert	Paste from clipboard.
CTRL+= or CTRL+- (CTRL + or -)	Zoom in/out of document(supported in major software)
CTRL+ALT+Delete	Last but not least, the original hotkey for computer reset sadly only sends you to a menu or sometimes unlocks computer. Now you just have to pull the plug, pull the battery, or hold the power button a few seconds.

Appendix B - Command Line Secrets

You can run almost any GUI settings page, properties page, or admin tool from command line. There is also many useful built-in tools that are hidden from the GUI.

Why you would want to do this is because you might be logged in with only user privileges and might need to run a tool on the side as admin to look or make changes. Also some of these tools are hard to reach or even hidden from the regular GUI. You can run any GUI tool as a different user as long as it doesn't require another instance of Explorer's user interface, that is opening of a folder. Some control panel features, like fonts, event viewer, and control panel itself rely on the current user's explorer instance.

All of these tools are located somewhere in the \WINDOWS directory. Most are in WINDOWS\SYSTEM32\ and, with some exceptions, most are globalized and should fire up from any directory(the GUI Start>Run feature seems to know where everything's at).

Note that some commands like those ending in .exe dont need the extension type in necessarily (of course) - classic MS-DOS assumes this.

CONTROL PANEL	
wscui.cplg	Security center
access.cpl	Accessibility Options
sysdm.cpl	Add New Hardware
appwiz.cpl	Add/Remove Programs
timedate.cpl	Date/Time Properties
desk.cpl	Display Properties
findfast.cpl	FindFast
fonts	Fonts Folder
inetcpl.cpl	Internet Properties
joy.cpl	Game controllers
main.cpl keyboard	Keyboard Properties
mlcfg32.cpl	Microsoft Exchange
wgpocpl.cpl	Microsoft Mail Post Office
modem.cpl	Modem Properties
main.cpl	Mouse Properties
mmsys.cpl	Multimedia Properties
password.cpl	Password Properties
powercfg.cpl (was:main.cpl power)	Power Management*
intl.cpl	Regional Settings
sticpl.cpl	Scanners and Cameras
mmsys.cpl sounds	Sound Properties
sysdm.cpl (WIN + break)	System Properties
control folders	Folder options/properties
control fonts	Fonts
control netconnections	Network connections folder
telephon.cpl	Phone & modem options

CONTROL PANEL(cont)	
control printers	Printers and Faxes folder
nusrmgr.cpl	User accounts
firewall.cpl	Windows Firewall
devmgmt.msc	Device Manager
control schedtasks	Scheduled Tasks Folder
ADMIN TOOLS	
mmc.exe	MS Management Console – Heart of all admin templates.
gpedit.msc	group policy editor
regedit.exe, regedt32.exe	registry editor – for low-level work
odbccp32.cpl	ODBC data source
compmgmt.msc	Computer Management - Management tasks root node.
diskmgmt.msc	Disk Management
eventvwr.exe	Event viewer - Displays logs of system wide or audit events
perfmon.exe	system monitor - graphs almost any measurable events.
secpol.msc	Security settings/policies
lusrmgr.msc	local users and groups
rsop.msc	Resultant set of policy
services.msc	Windows Services
fsmgmt.msc	Shared folders
comexp.msc	Manages COM+
msconfig.exe	MS Configuration Utility - Allows change/removal of startups, services
sysedit.exe	Configuration Editor - For editing Window's original config files.

HIDDEN APPLICATIONS AND OTHER UTILITIES	
clipbrd.exe	Security center
iexpress.exe	Accessibility Options
dxdiag.exe	Add New Hardware
eudcedit.exe	Add/Remove Programs
mplay32.exe	Date/Time Properties
ntbackup.exe	Display Properties
taskmgr.exe(ctrl+shift+esc)	FindFast
drwtsn32.exe	Dr. Watson - old debugging utility
winchat.exe	Windows telnet utility
Verifier	Driver Verifier utility
utilman.exe (WIN + U)	Utility Manager
narrator.exe	narrates any text
osk.exe	On-screen keyboard
Magnify	Windows magnifier
syskey.exe	System Security Tool

OTHER USEFUL PROGRAMS	
notepad.exe	Plain Text Editor
mspaint.exe	Plain Picture Editor
sndvol32.exe	Volume Control
mobsync.exe	Synchronize Files
calc.exe	Calculator
mstsc.exe	Remote Desktop Client
restore\rstrui.exe	System Restore - can sometimes undo a unwanted software installation.
Cleanmgr	Disk Cleanup Utility
dfrg.msc	Disk Defragment
charmap.exe	Character Map
hypertrm.exe	*Hyper Terminal* telnet program
netsetup.cpl	Network setup wizard
shrpubw.exe	network shared folders wizard

COMMAND LINE GOODIES	
ftp.exe	Command line FTP
systeminfo.exe	Lists system information
shutdown.exe	shutdown computer
chkdsk.exe	Check Disk Utility
diskpart	Disk partition manager
telnet.exe	Command line Telnet Client
runas	run a program under a different user account.
assoc	displays list of all file associations for current user. can also change or add file associations.
driverquery	Displays list of drivers
tasklist	Lists running tasks. add switches: -svc - show services, -v - for verbose mode, -m - shows .dll files
taskkill	Ends a task. must provide process ID #
ipconfig	Displays current IP settings. switches: /release, /renew, /flushdns
ping	detects other devices withan IP. `ping 92.168.1.4`
tracert	Lists destination IP and IPs of all hops along the way. ex: tracert <some distant IP addr>
netstat	Displays open ports for each running process

NORMAL BUILT-IN PROCESSES	
Can be seen running in Task Manager	
System Idle Process	% of free - nothing happening.
System	For system housekeeping.
explorer.exe	Windows Explorer - This is your file management system as you know it. Should not be stopped.
winlogon.exe	Account security
svchost.exe	service host - too many of these may indicate a problem.
services.exe	Indicates services (servers) running.
spoolsv.exe	printer spooler used when printer in operation.
csrss.exe	Windows process
Ctfmon.exe	Windows process
lsass.exe	Windows process
smss.exe	Windows process
alg.exe	Windows process

Environment placeholders for drive paths - Use the change directory command, **cd** to test these out.

Example:
```
cd %homepath%\Desktop
```
takes you to current user's desktop

Current Application data dir - **%appdata%**
Cur. Home Drive - **%homedrive%**
Cur. home dir. -- **%homepath%**
Shared home dir. --- **%homeshare%**
Temporary Folder. - **%temp%**
Installed Programs dir- **%programfiles%**
WINDOWS directory - **%systemroot%**

Intentionally blank -------------------------------------

Appendix C - Network Ports and Protocols

The physical computer, and network peripherals, connected by wiring, run software. This is what produces the fixed-sized frames of data, on top of that, specific protocol packages or packets, of various size, makes up the local network protocols, on top of that scheme, broadcast to the outside world with TCP/IP. And finally, high-level protocols can receive web pages, access a remote file system, send email, and so on. What i roughly described is the network layering that goes on internally. The OSI model is just that, an intrinsic model (and a guide) for how computer networking should look.

The 7 OSI layers of networking are roughly as follows:

7 – Application - Internet protocols like HTTP, FTP, TELNET, and others.
6 – presentation - higher level stuff.
5 – session - high level stuff
4 – transport - TCP/UDP, various data xfer protocols.
3 – Network - MAC to IP, SSL, Routers work at this level.
2 – Data link - frames, MAC addresses, and other low-level networking.
1 – physical - wires, connectors, electronic signals, etc.

Most of what a user sees done is performed at application layer. These high-level data transmissions sit on top of TCP/IP. Most 3rd party software will only work with layer 7. Communications over TCP/IP are like, to use an analogy, a phone conversation. a IP addresses and port number are like the telephone caller's phone number and line #.

Port number usage and what this tells - A data exchange can assume any port # 1 - 65535. Think of a port number as a handle. However by convention, port numbers are associated with specific protocols. iana.com has a enormous listing of these assignments that's freely available but who knows how relevant a lot of those are.

In the pages that follow is a listing i compiled of some protocols of interest.

Application layer protocols:

Name	Protocol	Usual Ports	Description
Domain Name System	DNS	53	Links cannonical/other website names to IP addresses + whatever server slot info.
Dynamic Host Configuration Protocol	DHCP	67, 68	Assigns IPs to network hosts. Back compatable with BOOTP.
Dynamic Host Configuration Protocol v6	DHCPv6	Client – 546, Server - 547	DHCP + IPv6 support
File Transfer protocol	FTP	21	Many online file systems use this.
FTP over SSL	FTPS	989, 990	
Trivial FTP	TFTP	69	
Secure File Transfer Protocol	SFTP	115	
Finger	Finger Proto	79	
Gopher	Gopher proto	70	
HOST	n/a		
Hyper Text Markup Language	HTTP	80	
HTTP over SSL	HTTPS	443	
Lightweight Directory Access Protocol	LDAP	389	Used to find and manage network resources.
Lightweight Directory Access Protocol over SSL	SLDAP	636	Secure LDAP
Mobile Application Part	MAP		

Network Time Proto.	NTP	123	Gives the time. Possible messages include 'client', 'server', and 'metric active'
NSLOOKUP	n/a		
Ping	ICMP>ping	7	the old way to tell if another computer is running on a network. Ping blocking prevents this.
REXEC, RSH, RLOGIN	n/a	513, 514	"R-services" - Obsolete Unix stuff - almost same as telnet - REXEC, RSH, RLOGIN
SOCKs proxy	SOCK	1080	
Terminal mode	Telnet	23, any	Telnet is the old ASCII text way of communication. Popular uses are Internet Relay Chat. IRC ports are: 194, 6665-6669, 6679-6697
Trace Route	ICMP>tracert	33434 plus	Pings destination endpoint and logs all *hop* names along the way
Voice over IP	VoIP	5060, 9750, 1071,10116	Digital Phone Protocol
Whois	Whois proto.	43	For retreiving DNS owner info
Whois++	Whois++ proto	63	A better whois

Email and Newsgroup protocols

Name	Protocol	Usual Ports	Description
Post Office Protocol v3	POP3	110	Protocol for receiving email
POP3 Over SSL	SPOP3	995	Secure version of POP
Simple Mail Transfer Protocol	SMTP	25, 587	Protocol for sending outgoing email
SMTP over SSL	SSMTP	465	Secure version of SMTP
Internet Message Access Protocol	IMAP4	143, 220	Another email protocol - IMAP4 works differently than POP3
IMAP4 over SSL	SIMAP4 or just SIMAP	993	Secure IMAP
Network Newsgroup Transfer Protocol	NNTP	119	Public Newsgroups (Usenet/Fidonet/whatever)
NNTP over SSL	SNNTP	563	Secure Newsgroup proto
Unix to Unix	UCP	540	UUCP was Unix to Unix mailing system for email/newsgroups back when UUENCODING was used just to send binary files(you had to do it yourself). Probably obsolete!
MIME	IME		Multipurpose Internet Mail Extensions - for text encoding 8-bit binary data for transport through mail protocols.

Almost all high-level protocols can be broke into 3 categories:

Transmission Control Protocol	TCP	any	accurate, error correcting data transport protocol
User Datagram Protocol	UDP	any	low overhead, raw data transport protocol
Internet Control Message Protocol	ICMP	any	Pinging other computers - Non-data.

...And those can be:

Internet Protocol v6	IPV6	IPv6(or "tunneling" hybrids) ex: xx: xx: xx: xx: xx: xx: xx: xx *
Internet Protocol version 4	IP	IPv4 ex: x. x. x. x *

* - x = 1 byte

This protocol is really important to IPv4

Address Resolution Protocol	ARP		Protocol that tells the network what IP goes to what MAC/Physical address. (Is even a reverse ARP proto called RARP)

Microsoft proprietary protocols - Some have to do with Server Edition's Active Directory, Replication, also DCOM, RPC, NetBIOS, network shares...

Name:	Protocol:	Usual Port(s)	Description:
Server Message Block over TCP/IP	SMB		The Protocol used by Windows Server for communicating with client machines and file and printer sharing(domain)
Active Directory	microsoft-ds, SMB, LDAP?	445	Active Directory Services and SMB Protocol - Windows Server (domain) only

MS workgroups, File and printer sharing, whatever.	NetBIOS	137-139	NetBIOS was one of window's greatest vulnerablility - enabled by default. 137=Port to find other MS workgroup peers
Global Catalog	SMB	3268	Global Catalogs are used in Windows Server
Message Transfer Agent	MTAP	102	???
MS Dynamic COM	DCOM	593	Dynamic COM - for remote work.
MS Exchange	Exchange	102, 691	
MS Media Server		1755	Media player related.
MS PPTP	MS PPTP	1723	MS point to point protocol
MS Remote Procedure Call	RPC	135, 1025	Supports a list of networked services that support RPC and DCOM.(RPC is for running code on someone's machine) 135 = RPC Locator
MS SQL	MS SQL	1433-1434	Used by MS SQL Server for replication and to monitor performance.
MSN		1863	MS Online, chatrooms, etc.
Remote Desktop	RDP	3389	Terminal Server / Remote Desktop. (default port # can be changed)
site replication services	SRS	379	Windows Server only

Universal PnP	UPnP	5000	universal plug and play. plug and play over network.
Windows Live	Windows Live	6891-6901	MS Online service
Online services (Messenger, Calendar Access Proto, other)	MSNP, CAP, other	1026-1029	MS Online services 1026 = Reportedly used for CAP, task scheduler, and other services.
Windows Internet Naming Service	WINS	42, 1512	Windows Internet Naming Service is used in client/server. (Ultimately is part of the NetBIOS scheme) 42=Replication of name tables by servers

Trojan horse / malware - IF YOU HAVE, YOU COULD BE HACKED

Name:	Protocol:	Usual ports	Description:
Bagle.H	n/a	2745	
MyDoom	N/a	1080	
Blaster	N/a	4444	
Bagle.B	n/a	8866	
Dabber	n/a	9898	
Rbot/Spybot	n/a	9988	
NetBus	n/a	12345	long established trojan horse software
Sub7	n/a	27374	long established trojan horse software
Back Orifice	n/a	31337	
Sasser	n/a	5554	

www.ingramcontent.com/pod-product-compliance
Lightning Source LLC
Chambersburg PA
CBHW022113170526
45157CB00004B/1623